Humber

and History

By Chris Horan

C000049493

Riverside and Waterways Tales Part 1

Winteringham on the south bank of the River Humber once boasted its own boatyard and a sloop can be seen on a floating dry dock left of centre. The haven at Winteringham today is the southern base of the Humber Yawl Club. The village was the crossing point for Roman soldiers heading across the river to Brough, though the line of the banks on both sides of the river is much changed over the years.

Humber Sail and History: Rivers and Waterways Tales Part 1, is published by

Chris Horan Editorial Services,
22 Priory Crescent, Ashby, Scunthorpe,
North Lincolnshire, DN17 1HX.

First edition 2010

ISBN 978-0-9567423-0-8

Printed by Fretwell Print and Design, Healey Works, Goulbourne Street, Keighley, West Yorkshire, BD21 1PX.

Cover design by John Jarman (Cleethorpes) with photos by Chris Horan.

Further copies of this book obtainable by post inc post and packing £15, cheques payable to Chris Horan.

Contents

Thames barges were a common sight on the River Humber with vessels heading up the River Trent to be loaded with coal at Keadby, where the Stainforth to Keadby Canal provided access to the pits of South Yorkshire. The village also had a railway coal terminal with a chute specially designed to load small river craft with coal.

Introduction: Lure of the Humber

THERE is something curiously alluring about life on the river and all the more so under the mesmerising spell of sail, be it a current day voyage or a journey back to the much romanticised era of yesteryear.

Mariners in the Clipper Around The World Yacht Race gulped in the salty air of the River Humber, before they set sail from Hull on their epic year-long voyages in 2009 but their experience of leaving the estuary was one with echoes through the ages.

The river, today a seemingly strange mix of industry and wildlife, in the past was the umbilical cord of heavy goods trade between the industrial cities of the North and far flung ports around the globe with their mystical ways and varying customs.

While commanding less evident history than the cathedral cities of nearby Lincoln and York, the estuary and its hinterland boast a rich vein of enthralling tales from reports of piracy, repression, heroism, quirkiness and catastrophic disasters.

In more recent years there has been the building of the iconic Humber Bridge, at one time the longest single span suspension bridge in the world, the building of which was a technical achievement, but so was the establishment of a crossing, mooted for more than a century, which also provided for the needs of sea going vessels heading for staithes more than 60 miles inland.

The estuary, according to Humber harbourmaster reports, is the busiest in the United Kingdom, but while the vessels today are much larger than in days gone by, they were more numerous and in many cases were lived on by their crews and families.

The rivers and local canals in the 19th and 20th century were awash with a variety of craft, including the Humber Keel, Humber Sloop and Thames Barges.

The pattern of trade is aptly described in an essay by Thorne-based keel skipper Herbert Rhodes: "The Port of Hull was the chief centre for the trade of the keel. Other chief industrial towns they traded to were as follows. Place an imaginary left hand pointing up the River Humber at Hull: the thumb points up the River Hull to Beverley and Driffield, the first finger up the River Ouse to Selby and York, the second finger the Aire and Calder Navigation to Leeds and Wakefield from Goole, the third finger the River Trent to Keadby and the Sheffield and South Yorkshire Navigation, the

The Hull and Humber yacht sails past the Hull flood barrier and The Deep.

fourth finger the River Trent to Newark and to Lincoln up the Foss Dyke Navigation from Torksey. We also traded to the ports of Immingham and Grimsby, on the Lincolnshire side of the Humber below Hull."

A celebration of the older craft involving the Humber Keel and Sloop Preservation Society, was staged as part of the 2009 Clipper Race celebrations which was quite apt following a flurry of restorations to sail of some of the few surviving craft of yesteryear, some of which a few years ago were rotting in breakers yards.

The HKSPS came into being by 1971 with the aim of preserving and restoring working examples of Humber sailing craft and reviving the skills and traditions of sailing the vessels.

The work of the society in promoting knowledge of the rare vessels also encouraged others to restore sails to their own barge type craft with two of

the square sheeted keels and two of gaffe rigged sloops starring in the Parade of Sail between Hull's Alexandra Dock and the Humber Bridge.

One of the skippers, Alan Gardiner, at the time of the parade commented: "These ships are a valuable piece of our history and it was a splendid sight to see them sailing

Alan Gardiner on board sloop Amy Howson.

Barton Haven was once awash with trading keels and sloops and the view here is looking towards the Humber with the Maltings on the right where today there is a country park linked to the west bank by a bridge leading to the old coastguard cottages and the viewing point for the Humber Bridge. The lower end of the Haven with sloop Phyllis is on the facing page.

together with the backdrop of the Humber Bridge. Although the weekend is about the Clippers, and rightly so, this was a big day for us to show off these workhorses of the Humber that built our region's industry."

I myself was among those who sailed in the parade on Chris Sherburn's keel Southcliffe and in 2007 was on the inaugural post sail restoration sea voyage from Hull to Scarborough of a vessel, the Spider T, which was missing from the parade, having been a feature of the 2009 World Harbour Days Festival in Rotterdam, Holland.

Outings on other vessels have imbued me with the pleasant feeling of tranquillity one can find when the modern day engines are switched off and there is a stillness which allows one to appreciate that in days gone by residents of communities on the North Bank and South Bank, could hail to each other across the wide expanse of water, which from its inception at the confluence of the Rivers Trent and Ouse, varies from less than a mile in width to almost six miles before emptying into the sea 40 miles downstream.

For those living inland to the west of Hull and to the north and west of Scunthorpe, the river with its tides provides a bit of an inland seaside and I can well remember my first sight of the river as a child on my way by train to Bridlington from the industrial West Riding of Yorkshire. Suddenly to my right from the north bank rail track was a huge expanse of water but the rush of eager delight was quelled by my father, who sagely advised his son the water was just the river and the seaside with its lure of buckets and

Barton Haven at its entrance to the River Humber, a far cry from the busy port of yesteryear.

spades fun, donkey rides, rock and fish and chips, was still some distance away.

The maritime delights of Hull, Grimsby and Immingham are the major ports of the Humber and while they are inevitably featured in this volume it is not a detailed history of their past but a work focusing on some of the smaller ports and villages which were once a hive of maritime activity.

The volume is not all encompassing and if you have old photos of the riverside and memories please send them to Chris Horan, 22 Priory Crescent Scunthorpe, DN17 1HX with an envelope for their return and I will seek to include them in any follow up publication. Please also include contact details.

The book touches on some curious lifestyles which would not be tolerated in modern times and also on the dedication and zest for adventure among enthusiasts.

The work owes much to the diligent studies of local historians over the years and local people who have related their tales and provided photos and stories from the past, without which this volume would not have been possible. I hope the snippets of their knowledge and my own will create a readable blend to shed light on communities of the past and the developing future.

The Humber remains a vibrant estuary with a major new port facility planned on the south bank near to Immingham and others mooted on the north bank.

A snapshot of traffic on the river in the 21st Century was provided by excerpts of a report by Humber Harbourmaster Capt Phil Cowing in 2007.

Humber harbourmaster Phil Cowing whose jurisdiction stretches from the mouth of Humber as far as the Goole rail bridge on the Ouse and Gainsborough on the Trent. He was one of the dignitaries on board the Phyllis for the return to Hull of the Around the World Clipper Yacht Race.

The report reveals the estuary is the busiest in the United Kingdom, with 16,216 inward shipping movements, giving rise to more than 35,000 vessel movements during the year.

It records the movements accounted for 91 million tonnes of cargo and more than a million passengers being moved.

In addition there were 6,247 recorded oil barge movements shifting 1.72 million tonnes of product between Immingham, Hull and upriver destinations.

An awful lot of management goes into the river, not only in craft movements but the environmental sustainability of the estuary, which is covered by a European Habitats Directive.

Management of the river is today partly governed by the European Habitats Directive and Capt Cowing's report noted Associated British Ports (the governing body of the river) had worked alongside 34 other relevant authorities including conservation bodies, local authorities, internal drainage boards and other harbour authorities on a management scheme to bring benefits in the way of wealth creation, jobs and the environment.

The continued development of the port of Immingham has seen a growth in vessels using the Humber, which was noted in Capt Cowing's report.

He notes the increased traffic around Immingham is due to the development of the Humber International Terminal, the Humber Sea Terminal and the opening of Immingham Outer Harbour.

"A major upgrade of vessel traffic services has taken place and includes the provision of an additional six operators to maintain the highest levels of service to river users. The £1.1 million investment has been used to upgrade the VTS infrastructure, the provision of AIS coverage throughout the estuary and an enhancement of monitoring and control in the busiest area around Immingham."

A traffic separation scheme exists in the Humber managed by VTS Humber at Spurn Point, in an attempt to cut down on collisions.

Figures for navigational incidents give an indication of difficulties faced by mariners on the river. Details for 2006 are recorded in brackets following those for 2007. Collision with vessel 2 (2); contact with vessel 8 (7); near misses 22 (20); contact with structures 74 (77); contact with floating markers lie buoys 5 (8); groundings, off same tide 28 (28); groundings, remain over tide 14 (19); loss of power/steering 99 (75).

Safety on the River Humber is also governed by ABP pilots, who board ships to assist them in the passage up the River Humber.

A breakdown of inward shipping movements for 2007 gives an indication of the destination of vessels entering the River Humber.

The largest number of movements were to Immingham (6,561) with Hull accounting for 3,796, the Humber Wharves 2,106, The River Trent 1,447, Goole 1,163, Grimsby 857, Ouse Wharves 185 and the Tetney Monobuoy 100.

In some cases the contribution is specifically noted, while in others it should be recognised in the flow of the text.

Attempts have been made to attribute source and in general copyright but apologies for where this has not been possible.

The Humber Keel and Sloop Preservation Society's sloop sails under and beyond the Humber Bridge, heading downstream on the river.

Thanks are due to the Humber Keel and Sloop Preservation Society and its members, individual vessel owners, the Scunthorpe Telegraph and Associated Newspapers and others, which allowed use of archive material, Alan Dowling of the Cleethorpes Chronicle, museum staff and archivists.

While the Clipper Around the World Yacht Race provided a spectacle down the Humber on its departure in 2009 and its return in 2010, the history of the Humber and nearby waterways is equally as fascinating.

Appropriately the Humber sloop Phyllis hosted the dignitaries on the yachts' return in the clipper race, including the Admiral of the Humber and the Humber Harbourmaster. While the race was won overall by Australia it was the Hull and Humber which lifted the John Harrison trophy in the final event on the river upstream towards Hessle and the Humber Bridge.

There was a great view of the vessels out on the Humber and the spectators were the real winners watching the yachts pass the ship shaped aquarium centre The Deep with the opening of the River Hull at Sammy's Point and then with the backdrop of the Humber Bridge.

The Clipper vessels then entered Humber Dock in reverse order to be greeted by crowds of onlookers and the music of the annual sea shanty and maritime festival, brought forward to co-incide with the end of the yacht race.

The vessels were equipped with all the latest in technology, a far cry from the days of those who handled the historic vessels of the Humber and a famed clockmaker called John Harrison, who for many years lived at Barrow-on-Humber on the south bank. His invention of a reliable and precise chronometer enabled sailors to calculate longitude and thereby navigate accurately around the world.

Finally, one last credit to the patience and tolerance of my late wife Gill, who although not as keen on the river scene as myself, was a pillar of support ensuring I had both time and equipment. After being diagnosed with cancer she hoped God's grace would give her time to see the finished product. Sadly her ship sailed too soon. God bless you Gill.

Author, Chris Horan, 2010.

Chris Horan and his late wife Gill on Lundy Island off the north coast of Devon in April 2010.

Chapter One : Parade of Historic Sail

THERE can be little more satisfying than seeing a hulk of rusting metal restored to its former glory proudly being blown through its haunts of the past.

But taking something which is well beyond its sell-by date and moulding it into a bit of a jewel in the crown takes both dedication and money.

It is a delight to sail in the Humber's sloops and keels at the owners' invitation or for a small donation, but such privilege belies the hard work of the restoration crew.

Many of the vessels now back under sail have been in a somewhat sorry state when acquired and have had to be a labour of love for those involved with them.

It has meant a pooling of skills from those with

The keel Comrade which was acquired by the Humber Keel and Sloop Preservation Society in 1974. It had been fitted with diesel engines but was restored to sail in 1976.

some know how and a thirst to acquire the skills from those who didn't know how.

The restoration work has placed pressure on marriages and partnerships but at the same time created a bond between couples and those with a common goal, to see history recreated in living form, affording a more palpable feel of what life may have been like in years gone by.

As mentioned in our introduction the disappearance of what were once common craft was the motivation behind the establishment of the Humber Keel and Sloop Preservation Society, which was formed in 1971, according to its records, by men who in many cases had worked with the vessels in the past and from their childhoods had recalled them being numerous on the Humber, its tributaries and the hinterland network of canals.

A Humber Keel Trust had been established in the 1952 with the intention of preserving some of the area's maritime heritage with the acquisition of the vessel Mayday, built at Richard Dunston and Co Ltd of Thorne, in 1900 for the Doncaster firm Thomas Hanley and Co Ltd. Even today the Yorkshire town on the Stainforth to Keadby Canal, retains a number of working boatyards, though the site of Dunston's is now occupied by a modern housing estate.

Mayday carried flour and grain between Hull and Doncaster up to 1941, but was then converted to an engineless lighter or dumb barge. There was partial restoration of the vessel with Stanilands of Thorne supplying a Norwegian fir tree mast free of charge, but the Trust foundered in its quest, run-

From the archive of the HKSPS: Keel Comrade became the first of the society's vessels but was still under contract to fulfil some 'traditional' duties when she was acquired by the society. She is seen unloading myrobalans, a dried fruit from India used for tanning leather. The transshipment of goods from ocean going vessels to smaller craft like Comrade made up much of the work of keels, sloops and engineless lighters.

Fred Schofield at the tiller of the Comrade as she passes along Hull Waterside as it was. Fred's wife Lilian is sitting aft and bearded Bill Wilson is in front of the chimney. HKSPS archives.

ning out of money. The dry dock at Stanilands is still used today to service existing craft from both the present and the past.

Despite the failure of the Trust, a Hull engineer, Cedric Lodge, suggested the establishment of a new preservation society, which became the Humber Keel and Sloop Preservation Society and was due to notch up its 40th birthday in 2011, the tenth being held on the former Humber Ferry Lincoln Castle, which was then at Hessle but after more recently finding a home at Grimsby was dismantled in 2010, though enthusiasts were hopeful to see it rebuilt in one form or another.

Today many of those early pioneers of restoration have passed on, with a new generation inheriting skills handed down, though a modern influence in new generation equipment in the case of many vessels has been utilised, creating in some cases renovation rather than restoration.

A particularly valuable work in documenting some of the skills, names and techniques was Fred Schofield's book Humber Keels and Keelmen referred to by some in the fraternity as 'The Bible'. However, one member from a boatman's family, who had learned much from elderly relatives, noted that there is more than one way to skin a rabbit, in other words in many cases different skippers employed different methods to achieve the same end.

The word keel is descended from the Anglo-Saxon word 'ceal' meaning a ship, and the vessel to which it was applied was rigged with a single square sail on a single mast.

The keel was a common sight on the River Humber, its tributaries and

The old and the new. Comrade and a modern yacht's paths cross as she heads towards Hull in the Parade of Sail with the Humber Bridge in the distance.

canals through to the 1950s. Many of the keels were fitted with a smaller oblong upper sail called a topsail and others boast a second topsail or 'top gallant'. The topsail was to enable it to catch the wind when sailing in built-up areas on the canals. The vessels were flat bottomed and fitted with lee boards which could be dropped from each side of the vessel to give it purchase against the water and stop it being blown about.

The Humber sloop was a similar type of essentially flat bottomed vessel which in its simplest form had a single mast but with a fore (stay) and aft sail (gaffe rigged). The larger sloops were fitted with additional bow sprit or head sails (the sprit being a length of wood protruding from the front of the vessel) and a topsail which was positioned above the main sail.

Following a donation of £250 from the Maritime Trust and the Science Museum, the HKSPS acquired the 61ft 6ins by 15ft 6ins keel Comrade, which had been built at Warren's Shipyard, New Holland in 1923 for Turner Carmichael of Hull. The vessel was originally named the Wanda but was rechristened Ada Carter by John Taylor. She was bought by the Schofield family in 1929 and was converted to a motor vessel carrying cargoes between Hull and the West Riding, including coal up to Beverley.

In his informative book Flying Sail, Humber Keels and Sloops, Michael E Ulyatt, notes: "Fred Schofield's father Arthur, bought her in 1929 in exchange for the wooden keel Galatea and £600 cash."

The keel was originally a sail vessel but was fitted with an Ogle 40hp engine in 1933, followed by a 21hp Lister in 1942 and a 31hp Lister in 1953.

Comrade was acquired by the society in 1974, returning to sail in 1976.

It was a time when barge type craft were being scrapped as quickly as the shipbreakers could take them, with the only reprieve for many being conversion to houseboats.

Fred noted the latter days of trade by Comrade before she became a working museum piece.

"I carried three cargoes with Comrade for the Society's account. The first was 38 tonnes of fishmeal loaded from a South African vessel and 44 tonnes of sunflower seed, loaded from a Russian vessel in King George Dock in Hull for Barker and Lee Smith's Mill at Beverley.

"The last two cargoes were myrobalans, nuts for the tannery of Richard Hodgson and sons Ltd, Beverley."

Both cargoes were loaded from the Indian vessel Vishva Bhakti in Queen Elizabeth Dock, Hull.

"Comrade delivered her last cargo on April 19, 1975. Within a few months all trade on the Beck (Beverley) was finished."

The Schofield book noted a pole suitable for making a mast for Comrade was ordered from a local firm which arranged for it to be imported from Gothenburg, via Gunness on the River Trent. Wharton Shipping Ltd, until recently in the family of the Scunthorpe United chairman Steve Wharton, confirmed it had been shipped on board the merchant vessel Marie Everard, and was expected to arrive on May 5, 1975.

Mr Schofield noted: "In early October the pole, which was to be made into the mast, was lifted out of the Beck, where it had been all summer, and placed on trestles in Hodgson's yard to dry out. Society member Jim Thompson started to take the bark off a month later."

The sails for the vessel came from Jeckells of Wroxham and and were made of a terylene fabric with greater durability than the traditional flax.

Bill Wilson and Jim Thompson making the mast for Comrade. Photo: HKSPS.

The rope for the rigging was made at Hall's Barton Ropery, which is now closed and turned into various units and a community hall. The firm reputedly supplied rope for Sir Edmund Hillary's conquest of Everest in 1953.

The restoration of Comrade, to her former glory, has over the years attracted the interest of major TV companies. but before filming immediately after restoration it was decided to have a trial run in Comrade, recalled in Fred Schofield's book.

"On Saturday morning August 14, 1976, without a word to anyone, we sent down the River Hull to the Humber to have a practice sail before we had to face the cameras. I was the only one on board who knew what to do and how to do it; the crew had not even seen sails set before that day."

It was a successful outing downstream to Paull with just the mainsail and then back with the help of the topsail. There were good conditions to sail before the cameras on the Sunday and Monday and on the latter a brief encounter with another vessel of a bygone era, which is now moored in Grimsby and featured elsewhere in this volume.

"As we were returning to Hull on the starboard tack the paddle steamer Lincoln Castle, crossed our bows, and the captain gave us a salute with his steam whistle."

One more than one occasion Comrade's path has been crossed by the Royal Family. The Royal yacht Britannia was in the Humber in 1977 for the Queen's visit to Grimsby and the Royal barge crossed the path of Comrade. On July 17, 1981, along with sloop Amy Howson, Comrade was involved in the official opening activities of the Humber Bridge. Fred Schofield at the tiller of Comrade was spotted by the Duke of Edinburgh, who gave him a respectful wave.

The restoration of the Comrade, just one of the vessels in the Parade of Sail, was due to the donated labour and voluntary fundraising of members and Humber area firms. The bulk of the work was completed by August 1976, but keeping the vessel afloat so it can carry passengers on outings and meet stringent rules and regulations means much has been spent on it in the four decades since then.

Comrade was the subject of a Yorkshire Television documentary 'Spilling the Wind' in 1990, featuring Fred Schofield, then aged 84. She

Fred Schofield and Colin Screeton with the Comrade in April 1990.

Fred Schofield at the tiller of the Comrade as she passes along Hull Waterside as it was. Fred's wife Lilian is sitting aft and bearded Bill Wilson is in front of the chimney. HKSPS archives.

had earlier featured in a BBC2 programme 'Past Afloat' in 1981.

With financial help from the Lincolnshire and Humberside Arts Association, the Humber sloop Amy Howson was acquired by the HKSPS in 1976 and was back under sail for the first time since 1939, in June 1981, shortly before the HKSPS held a celebratory 10th anniversary dinner on the Lincoln Castle on Hessle foreshore, on June 19. The dinner was just five days before traffic would start running across the Humber Bridge, spelling the death knell for the ferries which ceased on June 24.

The Amy Howson was built to carry coal for George Scaife at Scarr's Shipyard, Beverley, in 1914, later carrying parcels and oil seed. Her original name was Sophia and at one time she was keel rigged, switching to sloop rigging in 1916. She was bought by Gouldthorpe, Scott and Wright of Grimsby in 1920 and her name changed to I Know. In 1922 Barclays Bank sold her to William H Barraclough of Hull. Amy Howson was one of his daughters and used to live in a cottage a couple of hundred yards from South Ferriby Marina. It was at South Ferriby that restoration work was carried out by society members.

Much of Amy Howson's later trade was carrying chemicals to Barton-upon-Humber and oil seed to Yarborough Oil Mills on the new River Ancholme near Brigg. The mills were run by the Farmer's Company and later

The Amy Howson in something of a sorry state.

Living accommodation inside a sloop or keel was often limited, but cosy, with a fire and place to keep the kettle boiling.

by the firm Albright and Wilson, which had a major operation at Barton-upon-Humber. The mills were rebuilt following a big fire in 1910 but were finally demolished following another fire in the late 1980s and are now the site of a modern housing development.

The archives of the Scunthorpe Evening Telegraph in 1978 recorded the near completion of restoration work on Amy Howson.

"By 1968, after a long career, she seemed destined for the scrap heap. Then a member of the preservation society who had been a mate on the Amy Howson alerted the members this might be the good example of a sloop they had been looking for."

Closer inspection showed the vessel was not beyond repair.

"Members and friends of the South Bank section spent three winter months mending and cleaning the

The Amy Howson passes through the bridge at Ferriby Sluice. Work started on building the bridge on November 15, 1982 and was expected to be completed in four months, replacing a 50 year old swing bridge. A temporary bailey bridge can be seen top left. Humberside County Council estimated the work would cost £384,000.

engine. They scraped rust from the body, repaired the hatches and cleaned out the boat. The Manpower Services provided two workers to repair the floor and built steps."

Author Michael Ulyatt noted: "On Sunday June 14, 1981 Amy Howson sailed on the Humber under full sail for the first time since 1939."

The late David Robinson, a relief sailing master and secretary of the Humber Keel and Sloop Preservation Society some years ago relayed the differences between sailing a sloop or keel and other vessels.

"Sailing a sloop or keel is totally different to sailing a yacht or dinghy. It is the difference between pushing an empty wheelbarrow and pushing one full of bricks."

He said all the gear on the vessel was heavier, affecting the manoeuvrability of the craft and consequently decisions had to be taken earlier.

Mr Robinson said families in the past lived on their vessels and by the age of 12 to 14, they were already gaining experience of handling them.

"You do not get yachtsmen interested because they want something fast

The Phyllis in the Parade on the left with the Humber Bridge and sloop Amy Howson to the rear.

and ripping. With us it is more of a plod."

Comrade and Amy Howson, are not there simply for people to look at but for people to get real experience either as a society member, learning the old skills and those laid down for mariners today, or simply for those wanting to be taken for a sail on the river.

During late spring and the summer months the society provides a programme of sailings in the vessels from South Ferriby with both craft licensed to carry 12 passengers as far seaward as a line between Cleethorpes pier and the church at Patrington. There is a charge but it is good value for the time you are out on the river. It can be extremely pleasant but a little less so on days of bad weather.

Another of the vessels to take part in the Parade of Sail was Phyllis, which has, has been restored by North Lincolnshire based Kath Jones and Alan Gardiner, who were brought together by their common interest. Kath had lived in a Dutch barge on the River Thames in London and Alan was a skipper with the HKSPS.

Today the vessel, with its five sails, is a splendid sight to behold but it wasn't exactly plain sailing rescuing and restoring the 68ft by 16ft 6ins sloop built at Warren's shipyard in New Holland, in 1907.

Built for James Barraclough's of Barton. Phyllis is named after one of his daughters. The vessel was constructed to a design opting for speed over carrying capacity and boasts a distinctive aerodynamically tapered hull.

It seems obvious the Phyllis was built as much for speed as cargo and was very much designed as a vessel well capable of coping with coastal waters.

Government grants in the 1930s encouraged sloop and keel owners to install diesel engines so they were not dependent on the vagaries of the wind and tides. Like many of her fellow craft, Phyllis was converted to engine power and in due course lost her sails and rigging. She also found herself sailing away from the Humber northwards to Scotland, where in 1983 she experienced her greatest claim to fame as a vessel engaged by a Canadian team hunting for the Loch Ness Monster. Unfortunately, or fortunately, whichever way you look at it old 'Nessie' failed to raise his head.

The Phyllis in the 1920s.

One time civil servant Kath had parted company with her Dutch barge and was hunting for another vessel when she spotted Phyllis in a trade magazine.

Phyllis was in a sorry state and Kath literally saved her from the scrapyard when she bought the vessel back in 1998.

"It was pretty much a wreck and the original surveyor I asked to look at her said it was not worth his fee," said Kath.

Phyllis, which at one time had a detention order placed on her by the Maritime Coastal Authority, had been thought to have a paper thin hull, but this was partly due to a misleading diagnosis due to the use of inappropriate ultrasonic testing on the hull. A more traditional method of giving the hull a good belting with a sledge hammer showed it was sounder than previously diagnosed, though some repairs were required and it was taken to Buckie before being towed to Barton by the fishing vessel Benbola in 2001.

The couple aimed to have the Phyllis back under sail in time for her 100th birthday but the work was gradual.

The fore end of the Phyllis was virtually rebuilt and the vertical mini walls, known as coamings, around the hatches were replaced and a curved

The Phyllis on the left with the Benbola leading the way.

hatch roof replaced by steel as opposed to what would have been wooden hatch covers.

The support structure which would hold the mast of the vessel in place had to be replaced ahead of a new mast being made and a bulkhead was installed to accommodate a 180 horsepower Gardner engine, replacing the Lister 33 horsepower engine the vessel had been fitted with.

The foredeck was reinforced and a new anchor windlass was made and fitted on the foredeck. The deck ribs and the knees supporting the ribs were strengthened.

The hawse plates were replaced at the front of the deck carrying the hawse eye, to allow the anchor cable to pass through.

Alan, who was born in Whitecross Street in Barton, had studied motor vehicle engineering at North Lindsey College, Scunthorpe and the skills he learned in his early days helped him carry out repairs for less than it would have cost others to do.

"You were a mechanic but you did everything from rebuilding engines to welding, plating and cutting, besides mechanics."

Throughout the work on Phyllis both Alan and Kath had to keep working to raise the cash to provide what was needed for restoration. It wasn't until 2005 that the vessel found her way into dry dock at Hepworth's in Paull to be surveyed and to have her hull painted.

Then came the mammoth task of creating a new mast from the trunk of a Corsican pine tree which had been grown at Appleby, near Scunthorpe.

Alan used a traditional adze and draw knife to hone down the tree trunk to the correct dimensions for the 64ft 8ins mast. A photo showing the raw

Alan Gardiner honed down a tree trunk mast in preparation for it to be installed on Phyllis.

mast laid across five oil drums with an inset of Alan shows the sheer enormity of the task.

It was his mechanical skills which brought Alan into the HKSPS back in 1984. He had repaired an engine on the sloop Amy Howson and was asked to go on a trip in the vessel, which he did and ended up joining and becoming a skipper in 1996.

Even with the help of volunteers, to whom the couple are eternally grateful, the task of restoring Phyllis was massive and they are in debt to all who helped.

"Restoring a vessel like Phyllis needs both passion and a ferocious determination and ability to cope with endless frustration," said Kath.

But being on the river in a rare craft has its bonus.

"Bizarrely you feel you are putting something back. If you can bring that elegance back it is enormously satisfying."

Flying the flag for the Humber Yawl Club's 125th anniversary sailpast in 2008, when the Phyllis carried dignitaries on to the River Humber including the Humber harbourmaster Captain Phil Cowing and the Admiral of the Humber and Lord Mayor of Hull Elaine Garland, to take the salute from vessels based at Brough and Winteringham. Kath Jones (left) is holding the yawl club pennant with the then Yawl Club Captain Philomena Smith.

Chris Sherburn at Rawcliffe Bridge, alongside Southcliffe shortly before her new sail arrived.

Since being restored to sail, Phyllis, in addition to the Humber Yawl Club celebrations, has also been involved in the start and finish of the Clipper Around the World Yacht Race in 2009 and 2010, the former along with the keel Southcliffe.

The Phyllis, which is also on the Historic Ships Register, while complete on the outside at the time of the Parade of Sail, had still to be renovated on the inside to a design aimed for modern day living rather than an exact replica of how she would have been fitted out straight after building.

The fourth of the Humber area vessels to feature in the parade of sail was the Southcliffe, which has been restored by Chris Sherburn of Rawcliffe Bridge with backing from partner Beth Hardy and his Goole based family who earned their bread and butter working on the waterways, albeit essentially in the post sail era. She too is on the Historic Ships Register.

Messing about on the river is captured in the words of a traditional English folk song which conjures up pictures of lazy days in the sunshine. The song paints a somewhat 'oity toity' image of riverside life for Chris and family, who would readily accept their mindset as being more akin to communities influenced by the 'Where there's muck there's brass' philosophy.

However, there is a tenuous link for it was as a child skipping school to ride the waterways with his relatives that folk musician Chris perfected his skills as he idled away the hours. His time away from school also put him in good stead to retain the skills of a bygone age.

Chris's eyes were opened to the challenging and sometimes grimy job of transporting hundreds of tons of coal hewn from seams deep underground at the once ten a penny pits of West Yorkshire, to load on to vessels at Goole on the River Ouse.

He was, to use the proverbial phrase – 'now't but a young lad' when he accompanied his father and uncle on tugs towing and

The Southcliffe under way in the Parade of Sail in 2009.

pushing long lines of square shaped engineless pans known as 'Tom Puddings', piled high with the 'black gold' once used to power the nation and provide heat and warmth in the open fires of local households.

With the widespread closures of collieries since the Arthur Scargill led pit strike of the mid 1980s such scenes are now a thing of the past, though an insight into this bygone age is available at the Waterways Museum in Goole, where a hoist to lift and tip the Tom Puddings is being restored for heritage and tourism purposes.

While towing the puddings was relatively straightforward, the task of feeding them into a lock took considerably more skill. Chris pointed out many locks were not much upstream from a weir and if a boatman attempted to pull 600 tons of coal in fully loaded pans into a lock then he risked the danger of them snaking down river tippling, over the weir and pulling the vessel with them. The technique therefore was to take the powered tug closest the weir and literally ram the lead pan of the flailing snake of Tom Puddings into the opening of the lock, a manoeuvre requiring skills far beyond that of a Sunday boater.

It was while on his father's vessel that Chris, born in Wakefield on August 1 (Yorkshire Day) 1968 and brought up in Chiltern Road, Goole, developed his musical skills, playing and perfecting his mastery of the concertina, which he now displays on the folk circuit in partnership with Irish singer and guitarist Denny Bartley.

Chris's mother Eileen Sherburn (nee Martin) had run the folk club at the Royal Antediluvian Order of Buffaloes club in Aire Street, Goole, and Chris reckons being around folk singers had helped give him a natural ear for music.

Indirectly his father Goff Sherburn had also contributed to Chris's musical prowess.

"When I was born he was on Tom Puddings. He took them to Wheldale, Fryston, Kellingley," said Chris who accompanied him on the waterways around Goole, Castleford and Wakefield.

"I used to take the concertina with me when I went with my dad because if I was playing they used to know I had not fallen in."

He said it was very much a family affair for his father worked with his two uncles Ernie Sherburn and Harry Sherburn, who had both been deep sea sailors.

"In Goole there was nothing else, everyone went to sea, but as the uncles started having children they wanted to be at home."

Working the tugs on the canals and rivers was the only passage to life back home.

Goff (left) and Ernie Sherburn gave valuable advice to Chris on restoring Southcliffe and in handling her on tidal waters.

Chris gained an interest in folk music thanks to his mother Eileen, who ran the folk club at the RAOB club in Goole.

The South-cliffe sails past the Deep during the Parade of Sail: Photo courtesy of Lesley Everatt.

"They started on steam tugs but ended up on a diesel tug, the three cylinder Kellingley with a Lister Blackstone ship's engine."

While his father, who was tugmaster on the Tom Puddings, had all the skills of the tug powered Tom Pudding era, he had also picked up skills as a general boatman in his younger days and always described himself as a boatman.

Goff Sherburn had left school, aged 14, and started work on a West Country size barge vessel called Podessy, which had been a sailing barge but which, like many others had had a diesel engine installed.

Like many other boatmen he gained the knowledge of how craft manoeuvred in the currents of the tidal river of the Ouse, Trent and Humber and had a working knowledge of the sandbanks and which marker on the land a boatman should follow in order to keep in the deeper channels.

Those early day skills learned by Goff Sherburn are now being passed on to Chris who completed the restoration to sail of his vessel the Southcliffe in 2009, shortly before the Parade of Sail..

Although he had grown up with barge craft and the tales of days gone by from family members, he had simply taken them in his stride until one day on a visit to Holland, he was talking about the river craft there with his musical partner Denny.

"He asked me how I knew these things and I said it is what I am from. I came back home and started looking round barges again, that was at the end of the 1990s".

The boatman family heritage rekindled in Chris, had similarly been set alight for his sister Vicki Appleyard and her husband John, who had acquired the Southcliffe back in 1991 only to find the demands of their engineering business meant they had little time to work on the vessel.

Boats were often owned by more than one person and were sold on a share basis but Vicki and John had bought Southcliffe outright, owning 64/64ths of the vessel which had originally being a square rigged masted keel, before a 21 horse power JP2 engine was fitted in the 1940s. The vessel still has the same engine today and compared with its compatriots in the Parade of Sail suffered from a shortage of diesel power as well as less sail capacity, resulting in a bit of good hearted banter.

Chris took a leap in the dark to buy Southcliffe, selling his house in Colonel's Walk, Goole, raising £19,950, just £50 short of the £20,000 asking price, though at today's prices and with improvements the vessel would be worth much more.

He had trained as an apprentice car mechanic and had worked in general engineering as well as picking up many of the skills needed by boatmen, but the task of restoring Southcliffe to her former glory remained something of a challenge.

"The vessel needed a new bottom and it was half converted into a houseboat rather than as a working sailing vessel," said Chris.

His initial intention was to convert it into a working barge like those of his childhood but then he saw the keel Daybreak visit the Humber for the Hull Sea Shanty Festival, around 2003 and changed his mind.

"I just wanted to enjoy my childhood again with working barges of the 1970s. It is only after seeing Daybreak I started thinking, 'I have those bolts there and I have those brackets'."

It was then he decided to restore the vessel to something more akin to her original state when she was built in 1923 at Dunston's of Thorne, being launched on January 2, 1924.

"I got some engineering drawings and then started measuring up. It is a very addictive detective thing. You look at the plans and find the bolts which governed where the mast went."

He said he found the rivets where the mast went and that was it. He was hooked on a journey back in time afloat the 61ft 6ins (Sheffield size) vessel which boasts a width (beam) of 15ft 6ins and a draught of 7ft 6ins.

Chris said his lifestyle meant he would never make much money but he had had a great life. With money scarce he has had to work hard at doing jobs himself, aided by help from members of his family.

To make the mast he acquired a 43ft by 12inches square length of Douglas Fir from Summerscale's of Keelby, North East Lincs, that particular wood being used because it bends rather than snaps in the wind.

The main living accommodation on the Southcliffe is built in the old hold with the rustic panelling providing a pleasant atmosphere far roomier than that enjoyed by traditional boatmen.

In monetry terms the raw wood only cost £460 but there were many hours labour as he sawed, hammered and chiselled and planed it into a circular mast over a period of five weeks.

The mast had to be square at the bottom so it could fit in the lutchet mounting down below, which secures it to the vessel.

No-one taught him how to do it but having been brought up in a boatman's family and worked in engineering, he had an eye for the task and ingrained skills. When things went wrong on boats the problems had to be sorted by the boatmen themselves. A layman would watch in fascination but to him and others it was just common sense.

However, even today Chris marvels at the skills of his elder relatives with his father and Uncle Ernie working on the rigging, splicing wire shrouds and splicing and whipping ropes in the way of the old boatmen.

He has however compromised to some degree, using nylon ropes for durability on the basis that the the old manilla rope tended to rot and shrank in the rain. In the old days the boatmen tarred it to offer protection but that was not exactly user-friendly when using the vessel for people other than boatmen who would have been in their working clothes.

The historic Dutch vessel Texelstroom: Photo, Kate Smith.

"In 10 years time some of these skills will be lost and I am trying to keep them alive," said Chris.

He said in the days when powerful engines were available to some vessels it was worth remembering the boatmen of the past did not have such aids and had to adapt riding tides and reading the flow of the river to a greater degree of precision than nowadays.

The Dutch vessel the Texelstroom, which had been visiting England at the time of the Parade added to the spectacle on the passage between Alexandra Dock and the Humber Bridge, as did a number of other smaller craft.

The Texelstroom was built for the Dutch Navy in a shipyard in Amsterdam in 1906 and was a pilot boat in various parts of the Netherlands for more than 50 years, leading vessels from harbours to the North Sea. With a draught of just 1.4 metres she was also suitable for pilotage in the shallow water of the Wadden Sea. She was originally a sailing vessel but had an engine installed in 1918, resulting in a change from her original name of 'Botter No 1' to the 'Motorbotter No 1'. Following Second World War, in 1946 she was used to lay buoys in a fairway known as Texelstroom, off the Wadden Sea island of Texel, with her name subsequently being changed.

Texelstroom, now in the hands of a Dutch charity, is licensed to carry up to 12 passengers across the North Sea. She had previously visited Hull for the annual Sea Shanty Festival..

Chapter Two : Humber vessels revived

VESSELS in the Parade of Sail would have been joined by a fifth recently restored to sail super sloop but for gale force winds in the North Sea, which forced her into the safety of Yarmouth harbour in East Anglia.

For more than a decade the Historic Ships registered Humber super sloop Spider T has been the pride and joy of motor engineer Mal Nicholson and his wife Val, who by trade restore classic cars and sports cars.

Their privately owned vessel took something of a battering when they sought to return from being on show at the 2009 World Harbour Days (Wereldhavendagen) maritime exhibition in Rotterdam in September.

The journey over to Holland with a local crew was seen as something of a groundbreaking voyage by Mal, who set sail from the vessel's base on the Stainforth to Keadby Canal, down the Trent and Humber and the East Coast to Yarmouth before seeking to

The Spider T at the maritime festival in Scarborough in 2007, sporting her recently installed sails.

Setting sail for Rotterdam, members of the crew of Spider T from the left: Bill Tate, Mick Maith, Paul Coulthard, Clark Ross, Ian Murray, Stefan Plaziuk, Mal Nicholson.

slip across the North Sea under sail, subject to friendly weather conditions.

At the time Mal said: "The Dutch authorities are very excited about us coming, there has never been such a vessel supporting this event before."

It was also an exciting time for regular crew and helpers who had not only voluntarily worked endless hours on the vessel but built up sailing experience on her with sea voyages from Hull to Scarborough and to East Anglia in 1997, the year she was restored to sail, and Arbroath in 2008.

"The sacrifice which has been made to do this should not be taken lightly. It has been a monumental achievement and the women have been supporting us unbelievably and all the lads have pulled together," noted Mal.

The crew members on the outward voyage included: Bill Kirk of Kelsey Lane, Althorpe; Ian Murray of Crowle Bank Road, Althorpe; Stefan Plaziuk then of Wyredale Road, Ashby, Scunthorpe; Paul Coulthard of North End, Keadby, Steve Plant of Everton near Doncaster; Mick Maith of Old Epworth Road, Hatfield and Clark Ross of Arbroath, Scotland, though most, due to work commitments, would not be on the leg back home.

The early arrival in Rotterdam gave the crew the chance for a short break and to make the Spider T shipshape and spick-and-span for the World Harbour Days. Her presence was also of great interest to the Dutch who bombarded both Mal and the crew with a host of questions.

The vessel with its plush interior, hosted a number of meetings and was also honoured by the director of National Historic Ships, Martyn Heighton, who presented the Spider T with a banner of the National Historic Ships and prototype house flag.

"We were keen to fly the flag of National Historic Ships ," he said. "If you are going to have an official flag it has to be properly licensed and to pass through a formal process which includes the approval of the Ministry of Defence."

He said they were anxious to mark the presence of Spider T in Rotterdam as she was recognised as being in the top 200 of the 1,000 vessels registered with National Historic Ships.

Mr Heighton said they had no documented evidence of a Humber sloop sailing across the North Sea in a voyage like that of Spider T.

"They were not intended to go across the North Sea but they were intended to hug the coast. It was a very unusual voyage.

"As far as we are aware the Spider T was the only United Kingdom vessel in the Rotterdam harbour festival."

Following the end of the World Harbour Days Festival the Spider T had sought to set sail for England on the Tuesday before the Parade of Sail in the Humber on Saturday, September 12, followed by the start of the Clipper Round the World yacht race on Sunday, September 13, but weather forecasts indicating bad weather had caused her to stay in port. Eventually what appeared to be a good weather window appeared.

The plush Edwardian interior of the Spider T provides a pleasant home for those sailing the vessel. The interior has also served as a location for business seminars with hi-tech equipment brought on board for such occasions. The vessel has also hosted art exhibitions and a number of open days.

Mal, who said the sea was very calm on their sail over to Holland, reported it had similarly been the case on their way home on a course direct for the Humber.

They were happily under sail and all was going well until the weather broke as they sailed on a course towards Hull out to sea north of Yarmouth.

With stronger than forecast winds the Spider T was forced

to turn tail and head south for the safety of Yarmouth. It was an episode which saw Mal a touch worried about the safety of his crew and the ability of Spider T to weather the storm.

"It was horrific, the winds were very strong and the waves were high, it was frightening," he said.

The weather forecasts had been for winds of four to five with the occasional force six but touched force eight to nine.

"We took the decision to head south and get into a safe haven. It was really nasty, the rope snapped on the jib but the main rig stood up to it very well. I was expecting something to go bang," he said.

In addition to his crew of Mick Maith of Hatfield, Paul Coulthard of Keadby, Stef Plaziuk of Scunthorpe and John Edwards of Cleethorpes, the vessel was sailing with three Dutch citizens, Martin Clay, Iris De Kool and Nikki Hermans.

Iris, who had done a lot of sailing in her native Holland, said it had been a great opportunity to sail across the sea to England, but she and her friends did not expect quite as taxing an experience. However, with feet firmly back on terra firma she noted: "We met Mal at the museum in Rotterdam and we got on well. The chance to sail to England was a great opportunity. We had very rough seas but Nikki and I had a ball."

Master mariner John Edwards, of Cleethorpes, with the benefit of years of experience at sea, took the affair more soberly. "We had been watching the weather reports which stopped us making a move. When we went out you were getting 3.5 metre swells; we were getting pitched and rolled and it was wise to go back into port."

However, he said that by the back end of the week the reports seemed favourable to set a course from Rotterdam to the Humber but he acknowledged the change of plan.

John Edwards seen here on a later voyage from Keadby to Goole, following the installation of two new plates on the hull by white hot riveting. The process is pictured on colour pages in this volume.

The Spider T sporting her sails on the River Humber.

"We thought it was prudent to turn to the south and move to either Yarmouth or Lowestoft," he said.

John had joined he vessel from Palermo, Sicily, having been out in Egypt, but it was not his first outing on the super sloop, having been among the crew who made the Spider T's first seabound voyage from Hull to Scarborough in 2007, after the fitting of sails in 2007 after a 50 year absence.

The Yarmouth Mercury in reporting on the incident said: "Conditions became so severe in the early hours that the crew decided to divert course and head to Yarmouth."

The paper quoted Mal as saying: "We are extremely relieved to be here; it was some of the worst conditions I have ever sailed in and exceptional for this time of year.

"There were huge waves and we were out of radio contact for a time. The storm jusst came out of nowhere. The ship was really getting thrown around, but stood up to it very well – at times half the vessel was out of the water."

However, reflecting on the episode Mal said: "She fared extremely well. John said if the voyage did not prove she was seaworthy nothing would. "It was a good force storm nine, so we were suitably impressed."

"It was great how she handled it. It was great how stable she was, given the conditions."

However, the voyage had identified a weakness in that the existing rudder was maybe not as efficient as it could be, so back in dry dock at Stanilands boatyard in Thorne, as part of her routine maintenance, Mal chose to fit out Spider T with a larger rudder.

"I was not happy with the rudder. I knew it was a weak point on the vessel but when we took it off it was perfectly serviceable," said Mal.

The outward voyage to Rotterdam for the World Ports Days festival started from Keadby on Saturday, August 15, with a short haul to Grimsby before sailing to Lowestoft on August 16.

The weather they encountered was better than they had hoped for and consequently on Monday, August 17, they chose to set sail for Rotterdam, sailing into the sunset under a four hour shift system for the eight man crew. By Daybreak they were just 30 miles off the Dutch coast, but it was here they suffered their greatest mishap of the outward voyage, losing the vessel's weathervane and flag halyard, replacements for which were made at the museum harbour in Rotterdam.

From entering the river Maas, the Spider T, with her sails still up, was obliged to make progress under the direction of the harbourmaster but was the centre of attention with a pilot boat launching an inflatable to take photos of the unusual vessel.

Martyn Heighton.

The Spider T sailed past the sea defences and up the river to the futuristic Erasmus bridge, where the sails were lowered and the bridge opened to allow the vessel into the Leuverhaven and the Haven Museum, which is a working museum with its own engineering workshops, electrical department, blacksmith shop and appropriately trained staff.

The head of the National Register of Historic Vessels of the United Kingdom, Martyn Heighton, had flown from England to welcome the Spider T into the festival. He also chose the vessel to raise the new flag of the National Historic Ships organisation on Friday September 4. The vessel was also the venue of a semi-

Spider T prepares for the installation of its new mast, accompanied by followers and crew. Once work was completed it would be dropped into place by crane. Photo: Scunthorpe Telegraph.

The new mast is raised by the crane. Inset: The lutchet against which the mast is secured. On the deck it is visible on the riverward side of the wharf. Photo: Scunthorpe Telegraph.

nar for Dutch and British officials connected with the historic ship movement.

During her stay at the festival sightseers from around the world visited the vessel, including people from Australia, Canada, China and Germany.

The Scarborough voyage in July, 2007 was for the seaside town's SeaFest celebrations but it was the first time a Humber super sloop has made such a distant journey along the Yorkshire coast since the 1930s.

It was the first true sea voyage for the crew, with myself as a guest, since the installation of sails earlier in the year.

The passage down to the mouth of the Humber would have been routine for many on sloops and keels heading for Grimsby or further afield in the past but, it was something of a novelty for a relative landlubber to whom such small vessel experiences are now largely limited to the historic vessel enthusiasts or keen yachtsmen.

The Spider T, built at Warren's Shipyard, New Holland in 1926, with sails being the only means of power, on our voyage had the benefit of a powerful diesel engine to speed us on our way and as back-up should we encounter any unforeseen problems. As with other small industrial craft of its day, the Spider T abandoned sail and was fitted with a diesel engine in 1939, courtesy of government grant incentives.

The 61ft 6ins vessel, with a beam of 15ft 6ins, was one of the biggest sloops to have been able to pass through the inland waterway canal network from the Humber as far as Sheffield, the access being determined by the length and width of locks en route.

One of her distinctive points was the depth of the vessel and on one occasion she is reported to have carried 32 standards of timber. She was famed for having carried a load of 135 tonnes of outcrop coal from Rotherham to Sheffield.

Like many old craft she had been converted for modern day living with little thought given to her original exterior appearance or internal features.

Mal and his band of enthusiasts has restored the exterior of the vessel to provide an image fitting to the timescape in which she was built, but the interior is to a high class Edwardian themed design able to accommodate business meetings and passengers but also suitable for sailing.

The vessel had at one time been used as a centrepiece in a Rotherham police community project and by the time it was acquired by Mal it had been in use to ferry passengers from the Goole Waterways Museum by the Goole based Sobriety Project.

The old houseboat box-like straight sides and pent angles roof were raved away and replaced with a traditionally shaped curved covering of what would originally have been the hold or cargo areas.

A tree length was acquired and the mammoth task of honing the wood down to a suitable shape and size for mounting into the securing seat on board - the lutchet - was carried out by crew member Stef Plaziuk and hoisted on board at Keadby's historic Trent lock, which itself is a Grade II listed structure.

The lock at Keadby had recently benefited from a £2.7 million project

The canal at Keadby on the River Trent.

which involved the replacement of four sets of gates, the building of a new lock control building and other modern engineering works to bring it up to modern day standards.

In March 2008 the scheme at Keadby won a national award.

Laurence Morgan, general manager for British Waterways Yorkshire at the time said: "We are delighted that Keadby Lock scheme has won the Design and Construction category in this year's BURA Awards. I am pleased that the tremendous effort which our engineers put into this complex project has been recognised. They used their skills and experience in working with partners to ensure that the original features were maintained and new features were designed to blend in."

Keadby Lock is a scheduled ancient monument with the same level of protection as Stonehenge.

The cost of re-rigging and providing sails for Spider T topped £12,000 with a £3,000 grant from the Historic Ships Register, showing the importance of the vessel to those in the know. The overall cost of restoration far exceeds that and the work has been a labour of love for Mal and his team.

The inaugural sea voyage to Scarborough with a crew of five included myself and a boat dwelling lock-keeper, Gavin Graham-Park, as guests. Gavin lived on a 55ft former harbour launch Freedom in Humber Dock, Hull. He said he was not alone for there are 15 to 20 boat dwellers living in the city.

The crew members included Mal himself, Ian Murray of Althorpe, John Edwards of Cleethorpes, Bill Kirk of Althorpe and Stefan Plaziuk of Ashby, Scunthorpe.

The Spider T was built for Captain John Joseph Tomlinson of Thorne at Warren's shipyard and carried a variety of cargoes, including bricks and grain.

The vessel was acquired by Mal in 1994 when it was up for sale with a view to it being scrapped. What amounted to something not much more than a bare hull once fully restored by 2010 would be valued at more than £100,000 though running and maintenance costs are far from cheap and the restoration work, in addition to obligatory paid-for jobs, has involved Mal and others lending their skills and time for the love of it.

A seaworthiness report n the vessel noted it had been retired from service and abandoned in about 1970 and was subsequently bought by the Rotherham Community Project when some conversion work was carried out.

The report by LGSA Marine then recorded the vessel had been sold to the Waterways Museum at Goole around mid 1990 and was used for passenger trips for a period of time before being bought by the current owner.

Mal understood that at some stage the Spider T had sunk somewhere on

The Spider T in a somewhat dilapidated state.

the canal network in the Castleford area.

The inaugural sea sail of July, 2007 began early with a passage from the Humber Dock at Hull Marina into the River Humber around 6am under the power of diesel working against the flow of the six to seven knot incoming flood tide and one wondered how slow our progress might have been under sail alone, but then we aimed to achieve in one day a journey that in the past might have taken three.

We turned left, or to port, heading downriver, in the coolness of the morning, stealing past the opening to the River Hull with its flood barrier and the fishing centre, The Deep, at what has been known to generations of rivermen as Sammy's Point.

We were fighting against the incoming tide but mariners in the past would have ridden the outgoing tide. Our aim however, was to capture

The carlin hatches are fitted to the Spider T. Most vessels had wooden carlin hatches.

favourable currents as we left the Humber and headed up the coast. We hoped to make Scarborough while there was sufficient high water to berth in the harbour.

It was a fair but changeable day in which we would experience thunderstorms, bright sunshine and the fading light which near

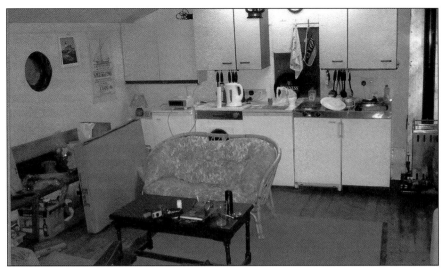

The unappealing living quarter and kitchen prior to renovation.

the completion of our journey would gift us with a brilliant sunset and a silhouette of Scarborough Castle etched against the fading light.

We were at Saltend by 7.40am and soon turned south east, heading down the Humber past the chemical complexes on the south bank where gas was being burned off, smoke released into the air and from which there was an occasional unwelcome odour.

As we made our way down the Humber, on the 87-mile voyage, we were still powered by the Spider's 180 horsepower diesel engine turning a surge propeller with a 50 inch pitch, moving the Spider T forward 50 inches per revolution.

Beyond Foulholme Sands on the north bank we passed the massive Immingham dock deep water terminal with mighty cargo vessels on the south bank before the river opened out with Hawkin's point to reveal wind turbines to the east at Easington across the flat landscape while to the south was the dock tower of Grimsby, Cleethorpes beach and Haille Sand Fort.

We passed between the lifeboat station at Spurn Point and Bull Fort, which is built on a subterranean sandbank on the northern side of the river, before spilling out into the Binks.

The sand spit of Spurn has been formed by debris washed down the north coast by the strength of the currents and once in the Binks the power of the forces of nature became evident with the powerful engine of the Spider T struggling to make headway against the converging currents which rocked the vessel from side to side, somewhat violently compared to the smooth passage down the River.

Heavy items had been stowed on the floor down below and as the pendulum swung the portholes along the side were intermittently submerged as we rocked heavily from side to side. One of the crew likened it to being in a washing machine. It was no place for anyone with a weak stomach.

For a good hour we seemed to be standing still, if not losing ground, but gradually Spider T overcame the currents. One wonders what it must have been like for the mariners of the past with just their sails to tack against the currents. They must have played a much more canny game but even with more time to make their journey, their skills must have been of the highest order, though many ships were wrecked along this stretch of coastline.

As the Spider T clawed her way against the north south current, the sea calmed north of

Members of the crew were still undergoing a steep learning curve with the sails on their voyae to Scarborough, in 1997.

Kilnsea as we approached the windmills of Easington and the decision was taken to raise the sails. "one must remember the crew were considerably less experienced under sail than they were on later trips to East Anglia, Scotland and the epic voyage to Rotterdam.

The vessel, with a sail area of 2,500sq ft boasts a main sail, a fore sail and a bow sprit jib with a topsail at the time still being made. The sails are thicker than boot canvas and raising them was no simple task. Recently added custom-made hand winches made it somewhat easier than hand hauling but the crew was still overcoming teething problems.

The jib and foresail were up first and

The unsettled waters of he Stony Binks seen through one of Spider T's portholes.

when the main sail went up the pull of the wind was felt immediately, though with tacking one's route was not quite as direct as under motor power.

Unlike the brownish silt-laden Humber the sea here was of a greenish hue, aptly matching the hold covering of the Spider T.

The storms were gathering as we sailed north along a clay cliffed coast-line to the groyned beached of Withernsea. We escaped the giant black clouds to the south but as we maintained six knots, passing buoyed fishing pots a bilious black cloud whipped across our bows, wreaking rain and fork lightning upon us. Rain poured down the sails and dripped off the giant telegraph pole of a boom, but it was calmer than in the Binks as we sailed on with the depth readings showing we had 31 ft of water beneath us.

Inside the wheelhouse a modern day GPS system assisted in the planning of our route, another piece of modern day technology which was unavailable to our forefa-thers.

Ian Murray tries his hand at fishing during one of the sun-nier spells on the sail to Scarborough in 2007.

At one point we dropped the main sail which with the crew still cutting their teeth seemed to be more of a rigmarole than putting it up. As we sailed north the weather improved and in glorious sunshine the sails went up again.

We were further out to sea from Hornsea and Bridlington than than with Withernsea so our main occupation became slumbering in the sun or keeping an eye out for fishing pot buoys.

Flamborough light-house was visible for many miles ahead but it seemed an age getting there. As we rounded the cave-potted cliffs we found ourselves of interest to the tourists out on a voyage to the headland on one of Scarborough's pleasure craft and as we passed Filey Brigg one wondered what Roman soldiers manning a watch tower on the cliffs above would have thought of our passing, let alone the thousands of sea birds whose nests we passed.

We crossed Filey Bay around 8.30pm and with sun dropping saw Oliver's Mount and Scarborough Castle silhouet-

The Zenitha, believed to be the sister sloop of Spider T.

ted on the horizon against a crimson sky.

The seafront lights of the South Bay twinkled before us while those in the wheelhouse sought to distinguish the navigational lights from those of seaside attractions. The entrance to the harbour is by the lighthouse to the side and it was a relief when we entered and found a mooring near the three masted Grand Turk, which was visiting for the SeaFest. Our sails were still up for show but open to spill the wind as we made our way under diesel power once more. It was dark and with the tide dropping it was good to have made our destination.

It had been an epic first sea voyage north out of the Humber under sail but one can only marvel at the skill of the sailors of yesteryear who made such journeys without the back-up of an engine.

For many years Mal has suspected the Spider T had a sister ship built to the same design and he said a visit by the now elderly Peter Warren, with younger members of his family, to see the Spider T in dry dock in Thorne, confirmed the theory.

Mal said, he had learned from Mr Warren, that the Spider T's sister ship was the Zenitha (ship 213 on the Warren's Shipbuilding log with Spider T number 216).

He understood the vessel had gone to a Mr Foster of Barrow Haven. William Foster owned tile and brick making businesses in Barrow and New Holland with both vessels used to transport the aforesaid up and down the coast. He understood the Zenitha had finished second in the final sloop regatta on the Humber in 1929. Another member of the Foster family had the vessel Madeleine.

The Spider T enjoyed a trip back in history herself with the replacement of two 16ft by 4ft sheets of steel using the older shipbuilding technique of riveting as opposed to the more modern welding.

The work was carried out at Stanilands Shipyard in Thorne, South Yorkshire, where the rat-a-tat-tat of rivet guns banging away was a common sound in the 1940s and 1950s.

Mr Nicholson said the end to riveting was signalled by the use of

Mr Nicholson at Stanilands with one of the damaged sections of steelwork removed from Spider T.

welding to build Liberty ships at speed during the Second World War. It had largely died out by the 1960s, though Rodney Clapson of the Barton-upon-Humber shipbuilding family recalled it being used for repairs to older vessels during his early days in the family's Waterside Road yard. The yard had last used it about 1965.

"It is very nice to see something like this happening. When they first started building steel ships it was the only way they had of joining them together."

Rodney Clapson on board the Spider T during preparations for white hot riveting.

Grinding off the old metalwork in preparation for the new plates are Bill White (left) of Thorne and and Ryan Johnson of Goole. Photos of the actual riveting are featured on colour pages.

Mr Nicholson, said: "The older method was less susceptible to cracking: It is a lot stronger than a welded joint, it can take a lot more stress."

In order to recreate the skills of the past he had to buy in some of the equipment from America and even there it was hard to find.

The technique involved Mr Nicholson and his team in heating rivets in a furnace before feeding them through pre-drilled holes while the rivets were still white hot.

The rivets were then hammered into place with a specialist riveting gun.

"I was excited but also apprehensive. We had done 100 test pieces before working on Spider T itself with a team of five men. "It isn't a process one man can do alone."

He said it involved one man heating rivets in a furnace. He then passed the hot rivet to a man inside the ship, another put it in position and a fourth applied pressure behind it while a fifth used the riveting gun to secure the rivet in place.

"One difficulty was maintaining the temperature in the rivet to make it workable. Every second heat was draining from the rivet and speed and accuracy are the key to the job.

"I am delighted to be finished but will miss the camaraderie of the team, which had a common goal to work well together to achieve success in very hot and difficult conditions."

Following completion of the work the vessel joined others at the Yorkshire Waterways Museum celebration of the birthday of the Humber Keel

Sobriety, whose name was adopted for a project which works towards improving people's social and economic well-being. The museum, which boasts a wealth of information on inland waterways can be contacted on (01405) 768730.

Daybreak inspired Southcliffe owner Chris Sherburn to restore his own vessel to sail.

In the account of the Parade of Sail, Chris Sherburn, owner of the keel Southcliffe, recalled being inspired by a visit to Hull of the Humber keel Daybreak, which is owned by Tony Woodward and his wife Sally and berthed at Staines on the River Thames.

Daybreak, which in days gone by had been a regular feature on the River Humber and surrounding waterways was restored to keel rigged sail in 1998 for the first time in 60 years.

She was built at Dunston's of Thorne in 1934 and had traded under sail carrying grain for Hanleys flour millers between Hull and Doncaster, but like many vessels of her era was converted to diesel engine in 1939, under the lure of government grants.

As trade died away the vessel found herself on the River Thames and it was there that Tony and Sally found the outlet for their dream home.

In an account relating to the vessel, written by Tony, he recalled: "We had already decided that a Humber keel was the vessel for us and we bought her with the intention of re-rigging and converting her to provide a home for us and our children.

"The process took much longer than we had originally envisaged, although we moved aboard to live in the original cabin almost straight away. The next 20 years were a balancing act between working full time and bringing up a family."

He said the restoration to sail of the vessel had been at the bottom of their list of necessities but in making changes to the hold they had always borne it in mind.

In 1996 a fire burnt out two thirds of the hold area, forcing repairs and acting as a catalyst to actual restoration.

"We had always planned to re-rig her but after the fire everything was such a mess and that spurred us on."

In his account he states: "Whilst replacing the original hatches with a new steel roof we decided to get the chain plates back on at the same time and from then it just gathered momentum."

The original sailing in 1998 was without lee boards, which help give purchase to the vessel against the water when the wind fills out the sails.

Tony had received training on sailing the vessel on board the Humber Keel and Sloop Preservation Society keel Comrade and had hoped to benefit from the experience of member Colin Screeton after entering Daybreak in a sail against other vessels from down south. Unfortunately Colin was ill and unable to attend.

"The lack of wind meant things happened much more slowly than we had experienced on the Humber Keel and Sloop Preservation Society vessel Comrade and once we got the hang of the timing everyone found life easier.

"When things did start going right I am sure I heard even Daybreak give a sigh of relief. However, whatever wind there was, was now decreasing and as the tide had changed it became clear we were not going to make it to the outer marker of the revised course we had been set.

"As we saw the second of the two Dutch barges turn and run for home we decided to do the same. The run back was positively relaxing and gave us time to plan our arrival and how we were going to lower the sails. This was just as well as it was under the eyes of the crews of the already anchored barges and smacks."

Tony and Sally brought the Keel back to the Humber for part of 2002

Ian and Leesa Murray with their vessel Onesimus

Ian Murray with a newspaper clipping showing the Onesimus with the TV stars.

and 2003 and also enjoyed a revival of the a mini Barton-upon-Humber Regatta with a sail down the river with the Humber Keel and Sloop Preservation Society vessel sloop Amy Howson and keel Comrade. The last full Regatta had been in 1929.

By its 100th birthday in 2013 the keel Onesimus also expected to be back in sail, boasting a number of interior fitments echoing the vessel's historic past.

If her lines seem somewhat familiar then it's because of TV film stardom The Onesimus was in the Yorkshire Television series of late 1980s/early 1990s, Stay Lucky, starring Dennis Waterman and Jan Francis.

Nowadays the vessel enjoys a berth alongside the Humber Sloop Spider T on the Stainforth to Keadby canal at Keadby.

She is the pride and joy of carpenter Ian Murray and his wife Leesa of Althorpe, near Scunthorpe, whose business, Redgates, is alongside the canal at Keadby.

It was through assisting Mal Nicholson on fitting out the interior of the Spider T, that a passing interest in the historic vessels was nurtured and blossomed for Ian, who like me, had been on that inaugural 2007 sea voyage under sail. Ian had also joined further excursions down to East Anglia and up to Scotland.

Ian had been scouting around for a suitable craft and had been told there was possibly such a vessel at Beverley. He visited the East Yorkshire Minster town which has a rich history of building river craft and fishing vessels, but rather than the vessel he had been going to see fell upon the Onesimus which was still there despite someone telling him the vessel had just been sold.

The Onesimus was in dry dock and Ian cheekily took a peep inside by the light of his phone torch and was bewitched by her intact skipper's cabin.

After tracking down those acting for the sale of the vessel and expressing the wish to keep her in the Humber basin Ian made an off-the-cuff offer.

"I didn't have a clue what she was really worth but said I wanted to get her back on the Humber. I came up with the figure of £25,000. I then came home and told my wife Leesa," he said.

Ian learned the vessel had been built at Joseph Scarr's yard in Beverley in 1913 and was made of Low Moor iron. She had been built by the Whittle family of Beverley. The deeply religious family had sailed her for three generations but refused to sail on Sundays and allegedly would sack anyone who swore on board.

"All I knew was it was an old sailing keel. What interested me was putting her back to being a 1913 square rigged keel."

The Onesimus is 61ft 6in long with a beam (width) of 15ft 6 in. She has a hold of 8ft and draws 3ft 6ins of water. She was registered to carry just over 63 tons but records show she carried between 100 and 118 tons of cargo. She was fitted with a diesel engine in 1936.

It was only after buying the vessel that Ian discovered she was somewhat famous when a previous owner presented him with some memorabilia which included clippings of Jan Francis and Denis Waterman.

Onesimus, a name from the Bible, was a runaway slave of Philemon. The meaning of the name being useful. Ian hopes to see the Onesimus restored by her 100th birthday.

The work of the Humber Keel and Sloop Preservation Society and individual enthusiasts in preserving and restoring historic vessels was applauded by the director of National Historic Ships, Mr Heighton.

He said ideally the organisation would like to see vessels restored to replicas of what they were in their working days but took the pragmatic view that this was not always financially practicable as the vessels of the past had to have a purpose in today's world to justify their continued existence.

"If something is to continue to survive it needs a use," he said.

However, he emphasised that any work done on vessels should not be irreparable so if at some time in the future money and circumstances created the opportunity for a full restoration then it could be done. As a consequence it was also vital to compile and preserve documentation on vessels.

Mr Heighton said the Humber Keels and Sloop Preservation Society had done some delightful work in the restoration of the keel Comrade, with its cabin and coal burning stove.

"What the Society is doing is fantastic," he pronounced.

Mr Heighton said National Historic Ships had been set up by the government to advise it on all aspects of historic vessels.

In addition the body helps to: maintain registers of vessels; provides advice and limited grants to assist in work on vessels; gives advice on the setting up of trusts in relation to vessels; assists in financial planning; gives advice to the Lottery Fund and advice to vessel owners on how to access Lottery grants.

National Historic Ships also helps: maintain pools of skills important to the maintenance of ships; keeps directories of individuals and bodies with specialist skills such as sailmakers, blacksmiths and dry dock facilities; it assists in the establishment of skills pools; it provides assistance with marketing including the establishment of websites.

Mr Heighton said there was also a need for steps to be taken so vessels were protected by law in the same way historic buildings are protected. He said at present there was no such legislation which meant in some cases vessels had gone to the scrapyard when restrictions would have provided time for those with the means to come to the rescue.

He said despite the obstacles two vessels, the Cutty Sark and the City of Adelaide had managed to achieve a degree of protection under the current legislation relating to buildings.

The Onesimus in her working days.

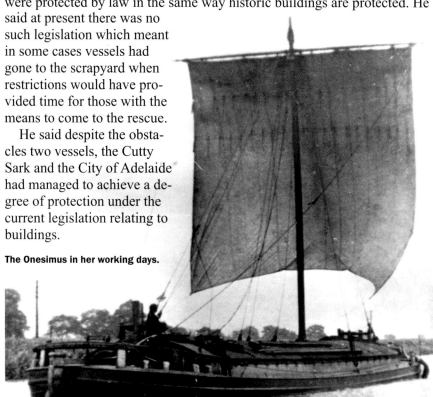

Chapter 3: Junk and yachts

A HUMBER-built craft, which in recent times sported an Oriental rig, is the New Holland built sloop John William which was away in France in 2004 when the vessel celebrated its 100th birthday.

The John William is the baby of Eric and Fionna Hutchinson, who had talked about possibly heading for the Greek island of Kythira when they and their vessel left the Humber in 2000. However, the vessel spent her time abroad in France, returning to English shores in 2009. At the time of writing she was in Torpoint, but hopeful of finding a berth somewhere in the Humber basin.

The former Humber sloop John William in her days as a square rigged vessel.

Recalling their time with John William, Fionna notes: "We bought him from Stanley Ferry Dismantlers, Wakefield, West Yorkshire in May, 1975 to convert into a home and business for us shortly after we met.

"He was about to be cut up for scrap and melted down. The only thing that saved him was the fact he had to wait his turn for the cutting torch. He was put in a siding off the Aire and Calder Canal, which acted as a temporary 'death row' for him and, no doubt, others like him, but we got there first one dark, cold, frosty February evening in 1975.

"For 15 years John William transported us round the British Isles, the Highlands of Scotland and the outlying Western Isles, then to Wales, before returning to his home waters of the Humber Estuary in 1990, where he remained for a decade, allowing Eric to finish education he had been unable to complete as a youngster.

He graduated from Hull University with an honours degree in electronic engineering and robotic control and worked in the university until his retirement in 1999."

Fionna, said: "The start of a new century and freedom from work restrictions meant that John William was free to move once more. At the end of

March, 2000 the lines were cast off from Goole."

The John William, measuring 66ft by 16ft 6in, was built at Warren's Shipyard at New Holland on the River Humber in 1904 for John William Barraclough. It was part of a fleet of vessels owned by the family, handling general cargoes including grain, coal, fertilisers and chalk, on the waters of the rivers Humber, Ouse, Trent and Ancholme.

The vessel headed down the Humber for what was then thought to be the last time before passing Spurn Point and heading down the coast to the south en route to the continent.

The Onesimus in her working days.

Fionna takes up the story: "His second life was just beginning. His first was over. No longer was he a motorised cargo carrying vessel, but an adventure-seeking three-masted Humber sailing barge carrying three bright green canvas, junk sails."

"Although the rigging had changed, the vessel, built as a Humber sloop, still boasted his faithful Lister air-cooled engine - all 33 horsepower of it.

"He was going south, then further south, until he crossed the English Channel into France. It was at dawn on Saturday, May 12, 2001 - 24 years less a week - after John William had sailed for the first time again after a long gap, that he slipped his mooring in Weymouth, Dorset on the south coast of England to head for Alderney, Guernsey and Brittany.

"As the sun rose in the eastern sky that Saturday morning the three junk sails were hoisted to allow this 'old man' to show what he was capable of even now.

"With a good north easterly breeze he picked up his 100 tons of iron and flew through the water towards the speck of Alderney as if his very life depended on it.

"Suddenly the speck of Alderney appeared out of the misty haze of a May evening bang on target. He had covered the distance from Weymouth to the northernmost Channel Island in just under 12 hours. He was far from jaded and finished. Oh no! He was raring to go anywhere.

"Anywhere finished up to be in Brittany on the northern coast of France, after a crossing from Guernsey to the Lezardrieux River in thick fog. So thick that the archipelago of Roches Douvres appeared out of the murk to stare at the Humber barge chugging along so close to its shores as if it was out of its mind. What was such a strange looking craft doing in these waters? This was the invisible frontier between the UK mainland and France and this boat was just about to cross it. Cross it he did without a backward glance, leaving the gaunt lighthouse speechless and silent perched on its rocky outcrop.

"On he went and on until the evening gloom lifted just enough to discern land ahead.

"That land should be the rocky coastline of the Cote d'Armor (rugged coast) and very aptly was it named. Rugged indeed it appeared to be. As John William closed in on the land, fighting an invisible battle against low visibility, a large beacon showed up to his right.

"This was the landfall beacon for the entrance to the estuary of the Trieux River upon which stood Lezardrieux, John William's hoped for destination that night.

Before he could get there he had to cross the tide running across the entrance and it was running fast. Eric, with all his experience of the sea and boats at his fingers, nudged his companion sideways across the tide, sideways and forwards until John William had crossed to the other side of the current and was entering the estuary leading to the wide river beyond.

"Like so many barges did when they entered the River Hull, John William came into France sideways! But he was quite used to that. He straightened his nose into the estuary and continued.

"The fog lifted, the evening sun began to glimmer through the clouds and the water sparkled. My thoughts were on Switzerland as we mooched up the river that golden evening in May. Eric was contentedly concentrating on the job in hand and John William, what was he thinking?"

Fionna said it was impossible for anyone to know but she would bet her beloved last chewy toffee that it went something like this.

"What is an old barge that has already served one life of servitude, over a 70 year span, doing here? Why was his life spared when so many of his contemporaries had died an ignominious death at the hands of an oxy-acetylene flame? Why him? What had he done to be on talking terms with Phoenix?"

He had been in the right place at the right time when he was needed.

Fionna penned a book John William: Barging Towards Junk, which relates to her and Eric's time with John William up to 2002. Although too comprehensive to be reproduced here in full it provides a fascinating log of their work on the vessel in Scotland, during which time the vessel along with sloop Phyllis, took part in the seemingly endless search for the elusive Loch Ness Monster.

Her book reveals the meeting of Eric and Fionna, was as romantic as any. Eric had always aspired to work on vessels and had left his native

Sheffield and found work with a Beverley based operation which designed boilers and steam engines for trawlers which were launched into the River Hull and fitted out down river at Princes Dock. It was here that Eric worked and forged friendships chatting with river folk and eventually finding himself work on a barge Sarah Teale.

According to Fionna's account of their times together, the skipper of the Sarah Teale taught Eric much of his early boating knowledge with Eric being an attentive learner. He later spent 12 years in the Marine Craft Section of the Royal Navy honing his seafaring skills.

In 1971, Eric secured himself a post of engineer on a passenger vessel on the Caledonian Canal. He worked on a vessel called Scott II, which, in 1974, saw the arrival of Fionna as an evening tea bar operator. It became obvious there was more than a spark between them and the couple would sit on the deck at night dreaming of the day they could do the same thing on their own deck.

Work on the cruise vessels was seasonal but out of season there was little else and come January, 1975, while musing over their future without either of them having jobs, and living in someone else's caravan, Eric decided he was going to acquire a boat and sent off a letter to a man who used to break up old wooden barges at Sammy's Point at the mouth of the River Hull, where it joins with the River Humber.

He didn't know if the man was still around and their hopes appeared to have been in vain until some time later a letter arrived postmarked Hull. The old man had been gone for some time but the letter to him was passed on and the writer imparted good news, indicating a vessel called John William was available.

The couple motored 500 miles south to Hull and then across country to a dismantlers close to Wakefield, on the Aire and Calder Navigation. Unable to see the vessel in the dismantlers in the dark. They eventually located her along the canal down a narrow offshoot. The couple later inspected the vessel in the daylight and then returned to Scotland and set about finding a way to raise a deposit of just short of £600 as part of the £1,750 needed to acquire the vessel.

There were some hitches along the way but eventually they secured the John William and by Thursday, June 5, the John William was back on the Humber. They made a brief call into Hull Old Harbour so an anchor davit could be mended, before heading north en route to Inverness.

Fionna recalled their departure from the Humber was on June 6, and coincided with Eric's 41st birthday. Bridlington was their initial destination.

Fionna wrote: "The fog descended as John William cleared Spurn Point, until visibility was barely a couple of hundred yards or so. He plodded on unconcernedly, Eric taking soundings, until by 10am the sun was out, the fog lifted and Withernsea lighthouse was visible five miles away. From then it was a beautiful hot summer's day as John William entered Bridlington Harbour in the early afternoon."

The vessel called in at Whitby before overnighting in Hartlepool, then a buoy off Holy Island before a visit to St Abbs in the fog. They then sailed northward to Eyemouth. The next day they motored across the outer end of the Firth of Forth, past Bell Rock Lighthouse and up to Stonehaven. They broke their journey at Peterhead on their way to Fraserburgh. With the time of their two week holiday almost exhausted they put into the tiny harbour of Rosehearty before sailing into Lossiemouth.

Fionna recalled: "The following morning, Saturday, the final leg of the mammoth journey got under way as John William left Losssiemouth harbour to head for Inverness. But as the day wore on the wind got stronger, the sea became rougher and John William was slowing down to a crawl.

"With no sails to set he couldn't make decent progress straight into a strong south westerly wind and with the tide soon to go against him, Eric abandoned his idea of Inverness and headed for Nairn on the east coast of the inner Moray Firth, some 15 miles by road from Inverness."

For the John William it had been an epic journey and they were close enough to home to make their jobs by the Monday.

The John William moved on from Nairn to an old distillery wharf in Muirtown, before being engaged to deliver equipment to Stornoway by the Scottish Telecommunications Board. John William's adventures were only just beginning.

The couple were anxious to restore the John William to sail but to do that they needed money and they opted for work in Inverness to build up their bank balance to enable them to fit out the vessel.

"Fionna recalls: "First there was the mast and some yards to acquire. Where could we find such a thing? Buying them was out of the question."

Having grown up in the Aultbea/Poolewe area, she knew a man who owned the forest near the water and having requested two large trees and eight small ones Fionna and Eric were told they could have whatever they wanted, provided they moved them out of the forest themselves.

Fionna recalls: "John William was taken round and beached on Gruinard sands, a little too effectively, as it took four days to float him again.

"In the meantime, with the aid of a wheelbarrow axle, begged from the village garage, the trees were fetched from the forest, to the roadside, loaded one at a time on the axle and pulled across the main road down to the beach. The two large trees, which would become masts, were parbuckled one each side and tied on to the side of the hull and the smaller trees were tied on deck."

It was hard work and particularly painful for Eric, who was viewed as a tasty dish by hordes of midges.

During the Autumn and Winter of 1975, Fionna and Eric worked in Inverness, moving the John William to Dochgarroch for fitting out. They had decided to go into the tourism charter business – a goal which became a reality.

The interior was fitted out to provide three double and two double bunk bed cabins for guests, with a saloon area and stairs leading to the deck. The rear of the hold housed their cabin, a galley and additional

Sorting out masts for John William.

toilet. Larch timber planking was secured from a nearby sawmill.

"When the weather permitted, the deck work was started too. The deck was planked over the hatchboards, roofing felt and bitumen put on top and a layer of fibreglass covered it all," recalled Fionna.

"The masts were put ashore on the towpath and the bark taken off. The interior work did, in fact, take almost two years to complete, as did the rigging. It was to be 1977 before John William was finally transformed. The bulk of the structural work took place during 1975/1976.

Fionna's parents had moved their boat business to Loch Ness and Fionna and Eric left their jobs to help them settle in and cope with the seasonal trade. One day, on their return from Stornoway, they spotted a craft similar to the John William in the canal basin.

The craft turned out to be Phyllis, another Humber sailing vessel, which had been brought north in the vain hope of getting work in the North Sea oil 'gold rush'. The couple bought the vessel on a bank loan using the John William as collateral. They were painted in the same livery and both were involved in searches for the Loch Ness Monster. As mentioned above, in due course the Phyllis was acquired by Kath Jones and Alan Gardiner who brought her back to her former glory.

Fionna said they found out Phyllis, built at New Holland in 2007, like John William, was a former Barraclough vessel. Phyllis had been named after one of the Barraclough daughters.

In the summer of 1976 the foremast of John William had been lifted into place with the help of a crane at Foyers. The vessel was being brig rigged somewhat different from her later junk rigged guise.

Fionna noted: "By late February 1977, the main mast was ready for stepping so John William made a return trip to Foyers to seek out the Hydro Board crane"

"The weather had been lenient, allowing Eric to get, not only the mast finished, but the six yards as well. Each yard would support one square sail, three on each mast.

"All the work had to be done by hand, the shaping of the yards from trees, the making of the metal fittings into which the yards went, called Goosenecks, the deadeyes for the shrouds."

She explained: "The shrouds were long lengths of steam-tarred nylon woven into a single rope that held the masts upright. The deadeyes were blocks of circular wood into which holes were drilled to take the ends of the shrouds which took much of the mast's weight at deck level.

"The shrouds were turned into ratlines to allow Eric to climb to the lower yards, where he had built a platform to stand on. All this work he had to do for each mast."

The date for the official launch of John William as a charter vessel was March 26, 1977. They were not allowed to be permanently moored in the Caledonian Canal, but John William and Phyllis found a home at Avoch, where they remained until April 26, 1982, sailing back to Foyers. It was there the couple acquired a third vessel in Eilean Dubh, the Kessock Ferry relief ferry boat. They intended using it in connection with the testing of remote controlled submersibles in Loch Ness and by the end of April, 1983, the Eileen Dubh was on hire to an American oil company to test its submersibles in the depths of Loch Ness. The vessel was later used to pinpoint the location of a Wellington bomber but the vessel had not been quite the commercial success they hoped for. To help cut their overdraft the vessel was sold off by the couple, when a mystery man turned up out of the blue with a cash offer.

In 1984 the couple returned to Inverness from Shropshire to find the John William had been heavily vandalised and set on fire. Downhearted they put her and Phyllis up for sale but only received inquiries from a scrap merchant and monster hunters on Loch Ness who had used the Phyllis the year before. The offer for the two vessels was a derisory sum and having placated the bank, Fionna set about selling Phyllis and subsequently an offer of £2,000 was made from a buyer who wished to take Phyllis to the Thames to live on her and use her as a workshop.

In due course both the Phyllis and John William returned to the Humber with Phyllis looking majestic with her recently restored sloop rigging. Further memories of the John William, which at the time of writing was expected to return to the Humber, are contained in Fionna's log on the vessel. The couple also produced a CD presentation on their adventures.

In addition to the old commercial vessels on the Humber, recent years have seen the growth of yacht clubs with Hull Marina packed with ocean-going vessels along with those in the Grimsby and Cleethorpes Yacht Club at Grimsby docks, maybe less well known are the Humber Mouth Yacht Club at Humberston, near the entrance to the Louth Navigation canal, and the mouth of the Humber, and in the upper reaches, the Humber Yawl Club.

A flotilla of yachts took to the Humber on Saturday, June 7, 2008, with a Parade of sail to mark the 125th anniversary of the Brough and Winteringham based club.

More than 60 vessels were out on the water to salute the then club captain, Philomena Smith of South Ferriby, off Brough.

She took the salute from the deck of the Humber sloop Phyllis and was accompanied by the Admiral of the Humber, Coun Elaine Garland (then Lord Mayor of Hull), the Humber harbourmaster, Capt Phil Cowing and

The battered John William, moored at Crinan, following the fire.

past captains of the club.

The Humber Yawl Club was formed in 1883 by members of the then declining branch of the Royal Canoe Club. The traditional Bermudan-style yacht most readers are familiar with has a single mast with a mainsail and a jib at the front, but the traditional yawl had a main mast to the

Vessels at South Ferriby with sailing boats on the right and a steamer on the jetty in the Humber. Photo: Courtesy Humber Yawl Club archive.

fore with a second mizzen mast to the rear of the boat with an additional sail to give greater speed and manoeuvrability.

The club's original base was in Hull, but Hornsea Mere and the River Hull were soon added as alternative venues with a move from Hull to Hessle Haven taking place in 1909 and finally to Brough in 1919, with Winteringham Haven joining the fold in the 1970s.

Following the move to Brough Haven in 1919, an established pattern of racing and cruising was introduced. Today members sail around Europe and a number of members have cruised the world.

The vessels which set sail from both Winteringham and Brough, gathered in the Broomfleet channel before sailing past the dignitaries who took the salute off Brough.

"It has been absolutely brilliant, I could not have asked for a better turnout and it is well worth just over a year's preparation," said Captain Smith.

"There were 63 out today, which was a really good turn-out given people are on holiday and quite a few are working on their boats.

"What has been really enjoyable is that it is not very often both banks join together in one event, other than racing. It was nice to see yachts of all designs taking part."

Admiral Garland in her first official duty in the honorary position said: "I am pleased I was asked to come and be here at these celebrations. This is my first duty with the ensign flying and I feel quite humble. People have been passing by and I have taken the salute. I feel quite proud. It is quite emotional."

She added : "It is part of history and shows the seafaring skills of the people who live in the Humber area both on the north bank and on the south bank."

Harbourmaster Capt Cowing, who has jurisdiction five miles out to sea from the mouth of the Humber, up to the Skelton railway bridge on the River Ouse near Goole and down to the bridge at Gainsborough, said: "It is an honour to be invited to receive the salute. I am particularly pleased to do it as one of our primary responsibilies is to ensure the whole of the harbour is maintained in a fit state for all who use it and that also applies to recreational users."

Capt Cowing, who is employed by Associated British Ports and heads Vessel Traffic Services (an equivalent of Air Traffic Control) said the harbour handled 37,000 commercial vessels with cargoes of 95 million tons a year, but the emphasis was for commercial and recreational traffic to co-exist.

"The skill and professionalism of the local recreational sailors is noticeably high. We as a harbour authority have always found them a good set of people to deal with. We respect their opinions and we try and get them involved in developments on the river."

He said the recent establishment of jetties for smaller craft at South Ferriby and on the Trent at Burton Stather, by enthusiasts, showed the vibrancy of the Humber and its linking waterways.

**An experimental amphibious tank on the Trent at Burton Stather.
Photo: Courtesy of the Tank Museum, Bovington.**

The Parade of Sail included a number of Bermudan style yachts, a catamaran, dinghies and an historic Humber Yawl, Leona, built in 1906. In the 1920s, when few vessels had engines, the club had around 30 such vessels with a second mast and sail at the rear to give greater

The tank landing stage as unearthed by enthusiasts in 2010.

speed and manouvreability.

Individual vessels display national ensigns and the crews of many on passing the dignitaries chirped: "Three cheers for the Captain, hip, hip, hooray."

A rather more unusual craft was seen on the lower reaches of the River Trent during the Second World War when amphibious tanks were tested with an eye on the invasion of Germany. Our photos of the tank craft are courtesy of the Tank Museum, Bovington.

During the war, much of the waterfront at Burton was closed to the general public but villagers had an inkling of what was going on. Similar activity must have gone on elsewhere but what raises the profile was a clandestine visit by Barnes Wallis, who in earlier years, had worked on airships at Howden, but more famously invented the bouncing bomb which

The new jetty on the Trent, at the Ferry House pub in Burton Stather.

demolished German dams and flooded Germany's industrial heartland.

While villagers have never forgotten the presence of the military in a small riverside community, the riverbank, with sea defences, has been much changed. However, in 2010 the ramp used by the tanks was unearthed by enthusiasts who hope to see it given the respect they feel it deserves.

In years gone by, Burton Hills above the riverside were a much loved day out attraction for the people of nearby Scunthorpe and elsewhere. Even today the hills afford good walking and pathways giving a fine vantage point over the confluence of the Trent and Ouse to form the Humber. The wartime site can only add to the attraction.

One of the amphibious tanks at Burton. Photo: Tank Museum.

Colour picture parade

The Spider T in dry dock behind the dock gates at the Staniland Marina, Thorne.

Colour picture parade

Heated rivets are lifted out of the portable furnace ready to be used on replacing steel plates on Spider T.

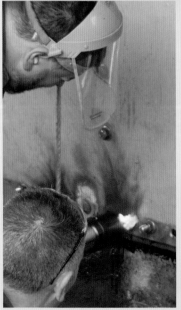

Mal Nicholson and Bill Kirk supervise the securing of a rivet while Justin Keyn, who helped pass and position white hot rivets from the inside of the vessel, in the confined space of a dust tunnel, takes a welcome breather from the hot and sweaty work.

Colour picture parade

The HKSPS Comrade sails up the Humber on one of the summer season sailings.

Left: Mal Nicholson in Rotterdam, proudly holds aloft a flag of the National Historic Ships. Above: Mal and his wife Val in Spider T's wheelhouse.

Colour picture parade

The Australian race winning yacht and the Hull and Humber off Hessle.

Sloop Phyllis and the Texelstroom in the 2009 Parade of Sail: Photo Kate Smith.

Yachts out on the River near Hessle with a Humber tug in 2009.

Colour picture parade

The Around the World Clipper Race yacht Hull and Humber off Grimsby.
Photo by Dave Moss. www.davemoss.co.uk

Colour picture parade

The Hull and Humber yacht off Cleethorpes in 2009. Photo: Dave Tilley.

Colour picture parade

Yachts in the Yawl Club's sailpast in 2008. Inset: The yawl Leona, built in 1906.

The Admiral of the Humber Coun David Gemmell OBE and his wife Moira who sailed on the Phyllis for the return of the Clipper Around the World yacht race.

Yachts in the Yawl Club's 125th celebrations with Captain Philomena Smith.

Colour picture parade

Two contrasting views of the John William in sun drenched seas and a snow sprinkled harbour tells much about the vessel's adventures to the inviting shores of Brittany and the chilly lochs and moors of Scotland. The cooler image, at Avoch, would make a fitting Christmas card. It also features the now restored sloop Phyllis. Maybe the card could have been sent to Nessie!

Chapter 4: The River in Context

DELIGHTS of life on the River Humber are nothing new for, in recent centuries, it has provided a rich life for the many who lived by it and used it to travel to cities inland which today we wrongly presume to have had little contact with the sea.

Places like Sheffield, Wakefield, Leeds, Lincoln and York had strong links with coastal towns in the past when rivers and later canals were their lifeblood of yesteryear.

Visitors to York may recall the last palpable vestiges of its maritime trade with barges loading and offloading on the Ouse at wharfs on the west side of the waterway now occupied by plush flats.

Newsprint was delivered by barge to the premises of the Yorkshire Evening Press in Coney Street up until 1989. The vessels, loaded with huge reels of newsprint, continued to be a sight in the city for a number of years after the publication moved its main offices to Walmgate and its printing press to a site adjacent the River Foss.

Next time you visit the city drop into the Merchant Adventurers Hall, which is not simply an endearing timbered building of the past. It had a purpose. York was an international city with links to the sea through the Ouse and the River Humber. In the 18th century York still had 60 to 80 ton ships sailing up to the city, but as ship sizes grew and silting of the river became a problem, the commercial viability of vessels sailing so far inland, waned, though gravel barges were still common in the 1970s.

Sail vessels back then, and even their motorised counterparts today, ride the incoming tide of the Humber upstream on their way to the railway age port of Goole, the Abbey town of Selby, through to the seat of England's second Archbishop at the appropriately named Bishopthorpe, a couple of miles outside the city. When sailing out of the city they would capture the ebb tide tide to speed their way towards the Humber and beyond.

York in Roman times had been an important port for coals and wine as were other inland ports, including Hedon, Selby and Beverley, which also enjoyed foreign trade in timber, wools and corn.

Unfortunately for Hedon, launched by William-le-Gross of Holderness, after the Norman Conquest, silting put paid to its trade, which was so vibrant in the 1200s it could reputedly boast a mile of quays.

The town's church of St Augustine was started in 1190 and today is known as the 'king of Holderness' dominating the local landscape.

The demand for larger ships and the silting problem led to some merchants establishing port facilities at the nearby village of Wyke-on-Hull. The settlement developed to become what today we know as Hull, the official title of which is Kingston-upon-Hull due to the acquisition of land by Edward I, the establishment of a harbour and the granting of a charter. In times gone by a charter gave a city or borough certain rights, mainly appertaining to running their own affairs. Today the honorary title of Admiral of the Humber is bestowed on whoever is the Lord Mayor of Hull.

The Lord Mayor's office provided the following abridged brief history in relation to the post of Admiral of the Humber.

"The jurisdiction of the Admiralty of the Humber was anciently defined as going to the mouth of the Humber, the suggestion is it went as far west as the county of the town, at least incorporating North Ferriby

"An inquiry of 1833 stated there had been Admiralty Courts held.

"By the 1447 Charter the Admiral of the Humber, for the maintenance of the Port, was entitled to all singular profits, commodities and emoluments of the office of Admiral. It would now be difficult to determine what those profits were but, it would appear that he had, amongst other things, the right of wreck, flotsam and jetsam, salvage, royal fish such as whales, sturgeon and porpoises, goods taken from pirates and ships of the enemy taken in the waters subject to his jurisdiction, although all these rights were diminished by the rights of others, such as the owners of manors abutting on such waters.

"There were also the receipts of the Admiralty Court which the Admiral held to try offences with regard to ships and shipping matters generally, the Admiralty Court at one time being held at the Woolhouse (or Weigh-house), in High Street.

In 1729 the master of a ship took a large fish alive in the Humber and

A whale, like this one on Cleethorpes beach in 1907, may, in years gone by, have been claimed by the Admiral of the Humber.

towed it to near Brough, securing it at the water's edge to his ship with a rope until the rightful owner could be traced.

"During a visit of the vessel of York, he being of the opinion that the fish most probably belonged to the Admiralty of York, a person named Hall, declared that he farmed the fishery, caused his

Splendid vessel lost at sea

MEMORIES of a mighty
ship which sailed the Humber and the high seas, but
was launched at Burton
Stather, on the Trent in 1866,
come courtesy of Alan Irons
and Winn Readhead.
The vessel, which disap-

peared in mysterious circum- **The Burton Stather mysteriously disappeared.**
stances, was built in the village shipyard.
"It's November 1865, the smell of pitch, pine, oak and tar hangs heavily
in the air around the Stather with the noise of adzes, handsaws and ham-
mering of fasteners into planks as the shipwrights are working on the
196th vessel to be built at the Burton Stather shipyard.
"At 154ft long from stem to stern, 27ft wide and 15ft high hull, she is
the longest vessel ever to built at the yard and what a sight she is on the
Stather skyline. As Mr John Wray, the owner of the shipyard surveys the
progress of his shipwrights'building, the largest vessel to date.
   The ship was built with three huge masts each rigged with five rec-
tangular shaped sails. There was a long bowsprit on the bow, with sails
from the bowsprit to the top of the forward mast (which are called stay-
sails). The ship was registered in the port London at 421 net tons, which
works out about 700 tons dead weight.
   She was built for Bullard King & Co, London to sail from the city.
Captain Warren took charge. He had captained the Silvery Wave, a 107ft
long, 192 net tons brig built at Burton shipyard in 1863 for Bullard King
& Co. They had three vessels built at Burton including Verulam, a 147ft
barque of 312 gross tons, launched on March 30,1865. By 1874 the Burton Stather was registered in Sydney, Australia, to W Andrews & Co of
Sydney and the Captain was George Carphin
   In September 1876 she headed out of Newcastle, NSW, bound for
Hong Kong. Nothing was heard of her again. She was presumed lost in
the South China Sea. It seems she had a stormy end close to Rossel Island Papua New Guinea. On the island's reef are five large anchors one
being the British Trotman design. The inhabitants of the island had copper sheathing on the roofs of their huts and blue and white enamelware
as early as 1902, from the shipwreck.

men to secure the fish and threatened any who dared to meddle with it. William Fenwick, the then Mayor of Kingston-upon-Hull, and Admiral of the Humber, intervened with his men, who secured the fish by the tail, and towed it to Hull.

The man Hall, brought an action against Mayor Fenwick and others for trespass. Hall lost his case and the success of Mayor Fenwick's defence, based on his rights as Admiral of the Humber, is interesting and, perhaps, of peculiar interest are the grounds of complaint of trespass which included damage to goods, fish oil, fish blubber and "lying dead there" one blubber fish, one oil fish and one sea fish."

On June 2, 1737 the Bench ordered "that Mr Mayor as Admiral of the Humber, shall exercise his Admiral jurisdiction on the River Humber at the Corporation's expense this summer and that a flag be provided with the Admiralty Arms upon it."

It is thought the flag flown today by the Amiral will be of a similar design to the 1737 flag.

"The powers, rights and jurisdiction of the Admiral continued in existence until repealed in 1835. The power of election under the Charter, however, remained and continues unimpaired.

"The office, therefore, survives today as one of those traditional offices in which the City may take pride as a symbol of its ancient power and glory, and which one may perhaps say has merely been adapted to modern necessities, growing enormously in some directions, diminishing in others.

"The Admiralty of the Humber remains as a title and dignity, carrying with it no responsibilities and no privileges except that calls upon the Lord Mayor by the Captains of visiting vessels, both merchant and naval, have a special significance in that the Lord Mayor is still elected and rightly bears the title "Admiral of the Humber".

"Indeed, as a courtesy but not as of right, the Lord Mayor in returning the courtesy visits, has his flag worn by the merchant ships visited and in visiting naval vessels. He may be, and commonly is, piped aboard and his flag may be worn, although the latter perhaps, on a question of strict procedure and etiquette, may only be so worn with the consent of the appropriate Naval Commander in Chief."

By the end of the 1700s Hull, once overshadowed on the Humber by the south bank haven of Barton, had become the third largest port in England. It was also known for shipbuilding and whaling but in more recent times was built on fishing, with Hull trawlers being caught up in the Icelandic Cod Wars, which raged from the late 1950s and into the 1970s.

The history of Hull and other ports on the Humber could more than fill a book in themselves so this work gives but a taster of the full picture of the busy estuary.

Spurn Point, at the outlet of the Humber, has not always been where it is today but has moved inland with erosion of the Holderness coastline due to the powerful waters of the North Sea (referred to by some as the German Sea), combined with the north to south current of the coastal waters.

Sea defences have been built along the coast but the modern day perspective tends to follow the philosophy that man cannot hold back the Kraken and should let nature take its course.

Even without global warming, Spurn has been breached on several occasions and future generations along the Humber will discover life anew once the huge sand bar has disappeared beneath the waves.

There is widespread sea erosion along the coast from Bridlington southward which has both added to the deposits at Spurn but washed away communities of the past like Ravenspur and the Houses of Parliament borough constituency of Ravensrodd or Ravenser Odd, which in 1295 had two members of Parliament but was abolished as a constituency in 1337.

One source suggests the sandbanks on which the town was built shifted in the 1400s and it was entirely swept away.

Ravenspur or Ravenspurgh is also mentioned in three Shakespearian plays, Richard II, Henry IV and Henry VI. Notes of the plays describe it as having disappeared, or been submerged under the sea.

Researches into the history of Kilnsea, which is at the head of Spurn Point, say its exact location was not known but note from old documents that Henry IV landed there in 1399 and Edward IV in 1471.

Such landings would not have been unusual and include a reported visit by royalty to Adlingfleet, upstream at the head of the River Humber near the confluence of the River Trent and on the course of the now diverted River Don.

The wildlife peninsular is a vital link in the management of

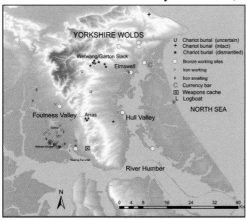

An archaeological map of the Humber and surrounding valleys gives an indication of large tracts of land submerged in the past. Photo courtesy Sean Spencer, www.hullnews.co.uk.©Sean Spencer/Hull News & Pictures Ltd.

Spurn Point was once a popular day trip destination from Cleethorpes and outings on the river as illustrated by a line drawing souvenir card produced by a photographer from the Lincs resort.

the busy River Humber and is the home of the only full-time lifeboatmen in Britain, who celebrated a 200-year presence at the tip of the peninsula during 2000.

Widespread flooding in parts of Hull and on the south bank of the river in 2007, although due to surface water run-off, showed the vulnerability to flooding of low lying land which through networks of dykes and pumping stations has been reclaimed from swamplands over the centuries.

The River Humber, born through the confluence of the Trent and Ouse, opens out to be almost six miles wide at one point and at low tide can be seen to be a shallow watercourse aside from the main channel. The river's terrain, favoured the essentially flat bottomed boat which in earlier days was capable of penetrating inland through shallow swampland settlements.

Following the ice-age a huge lake was created at the head of the Humber. Visitors to todays landscape have likened it to driving across the bed of a sea, which is hardly surprising as much of it was, albeit a freshwater lake created during the ice-age.

The area between Scunthorpe and Doncaster was under water but for sporadic islands, including the Isle of Axholme, famed as the birthplace of the founders of Methodism, John and Charles Wesley, of Epworth.

Much of the land around Hatfield, Thorne and Crowle has until recently been an area of peat extraction with the peat formed from the boglands of the past.

Conservationists have successfully fought a battle to end production and establish environmental protection for the peat moors.

Large tracts of land around Snaith and Selby were also under water and if current predictions on global warming inspired rises in sea levels are to be believed then these areas along with the more significant ports of Immingham, Grimsby and Hull, will also become lost submerged settlements.

In preceding centuries the emphasis has been on protecting settlements with coastal defences and reclaiming land by draining of marshlands. The modern view is somewhat more laissez faire, as reported in the Yorkshire Post in December 2009. The paper's headline on the affair was "Leave crumbling coast to the sea, shore plan urges."

The paper's article noted consultations had started on a "no active intervention policy"

"The number two shoreline management plan – which cost more than £300,000 – draws strikingly similar conclusions to a report 10 years ago."

The report covers the coast between Flamborough Head in East Yorkshire and Gibraltar Point in Lincolnshire.

Bridlington, Hornsea, Mappleton, Withernsea and the Dimlington and Easington gas terminals will be protected with some additional defences to stop the sea creeping round the back.

The draft says defending the whole coast would stop coarse sand and gravel eroded from the cliffs being carried southwards to maintain Spurn Head, which in turn defends Grimsby and Cleethorpes, as well as building up mudflat buffers protecting settlements and land along the estuary.

Small craft in Stone Creek, Sunk Island.

"Fine sand travelling across the Humber also builds up the wide sand beaches of Lincolnshire, a natural coastal defence."

The report says that around the Humber the current defence point will be held between Easington Road and Stone Creek but with possible limited managed realignment to ensure sustainable flood defences and meet the requirements of environmental legislation. From East Immingham to Cleethorpes the defences would stay in their current positions.

There has been talk of the tip of Spurn being left to become an island, though according to past records it has intermittently been so in the past. Should this eventuality arise then it is probable the lifeboat services for the Humber would be moved across the river to Cleethorpes.

Use of the River Humber as a thoroughfare for trade are evident in archaeological finds of vessels from the past, which include boats along the valley of the south bank Humber tributary of the River Ancholme and by the Humber settlement of North Ferriby.

One of the major finds, which survived for centuries in the marshlands around Brigg, was a 13.5 metre long log boat unearthed at Brigg on April 20, 1886, during excavations for a gasworks.

The boat, dating back to the 9th Century BC, had a width of 1.9 metres to 1.72 metres with sides a metre high. It was capable of accommodating 26 people kneeling down with another two standing.

The boat was put on display at Brigg with people paying to see it, but it was eventually taken to Hull Museum, where it met an unfortunate end in a German bombing raid in 1942.

The former principal keeper of archaeology and Natural History at North Lincolnshire Museum, Dr Kevin Leahy, said: "It was the biggest boat ever found in the British Isles."

He said the vessel had been made from a single oak log with the front end shaped appropriately for it to cut through the water. At the rear, or stern, it had been fitted with a board, fed down a groove in the wood.

At the front of the Brigg boat were two bosses (carved protrusions) representing eyes, creating the image of a strange water living creature, maybe the beast of the marshes.

The historic Brigg boat, which sadly, was destroyed in a German bombing raid on Hull, during the Second World War.

Another relic nearby, was also unearthed in 1886, near

AN exhibition image featuring he Hasholme boat, photo: courtesy Sean Spencer, www.hull-news.co.uk.©Sean Spencer/Hull News & Pictures Ltd.

the point of Island Carr. Initially described as a raft, it was a Bronze Age plank built boat dating from 870 BC.

Records note the vessel's planks had wooden cleats or protrusions which helped to bind them together with withies (flexible branch like willow) and moss was used as caulking to block the passage of water between planks. A thin strip of wood or lath was used to cover the join. The Brigg raft boat measured 12 metres long with a beam of 2.3 metres. The vessel was re-buried but in 1973 was reported to have been sent to the National Maritime Museum.

A boat from the 11th Century BC was found at Appleby, between Brigg and South Ferriby, on May 7, 1943, in the bed of the meandering old River Ancholme, a new river course having been created as part of drainage work.

Remains of the Appleby boat have been displayed behind glass at the North Lincolnshire Museum in Oswald Road, Scunthorpe.

In 1926 a coracle and skeleton were found at South Ferriby while in 1810 a 50ft long by 4ft boat was found in the River Eau in Scotter, the river being a lower tributary of the River Trent along which a 40ft by 4ft wide vessel was unearthed at East Ferry in 1811. Further north a raft with wooden finishing pegs was found at Greenhoe, Yaddlethorpe in 1815 and a log boat at Messingham in 1954.

Three boats found at North Ferriby have also been unearthed, with the first found in 1937 by Ted Wright, being dated at 1890 BC to 700 BC. The vessel was 13.17 metres long with a beam (width) of 5.6 metres. One end of the boat was virually complete with the other end missing.

A second boat, found on the Humber foreshore near the first, in 1940 and later excavated with the first in 1946, was dated as from 1930 BC to 1750 BC and the third which was unearthed in 1963, as 2030 BC to 1780 BC. Both this and the first boat were taken to the National Maritime Museum at Greenwich.

The third vessel had room for 18 paddlers with nine timbers or thwarts across the boat. The vessel was 16 metres long and large enough to carry people or animals.

A website for the Ferriby Boats (www,ferribyboats.co.uk) notes the first more complete vessel consisted of a flat but 'rockered' structure of three strakes with the keel strake being of two planks joined amid-

The excavated Hasholme boat. Photo: Sean Spencer, www.hullnews.co.uk.©Sean Spencer/Hull News & Pictures Ltd.

ships with the remaining end and presumably the missing end also, shaped in an upwards curve.

On either side were outer bottom strakes (planks of wood running along the length of the boat) each with a plank of 35ft curved on the outer edges.

The bottom structure was braced laterally by transverse timbers passing through cleats shaped integrally on the planks. The planks were three to four inches thick broadening to six to eight inches amidships. They were stitched together with withies of yew branch at nine to 12 inch intervals.

As with the Brigg raft boat the seams were caulked by moss and capped by oak laths. The interlocking seams were so shaped to protect the stitching when the boat grounded.

It is estimated the vessel could have accommodated 18 paddlers with cargo of 4.5 tons, making the total weight in the craft up to 11 tons. The vessel would have achieved a speed of around six knots, today's tides generally being between three and five knots.

The Humber estuary has long served as a divide between governing bodies with the loyalties of those on the north bank to the old county of Yorkshire and those on the south bank to Lincolnshire, having put paid to the new authority of Humberside created in 1974, despite the opening of the Humber Bridge, featured later. The fleeting Humberside was dismembered into unitary authorities in 1996 with Hull and East Yorkshire on the north bank and North Lincolnshire and North East Lincolnshire on the south bank, though joint police and fire authorities survived.

The building of the Humber Bridge, completed in 1981, was expected to act as a unifying force and had the county authority been called East Yorkshire and North Lincolnshire it may well have survived.

Natural and political divide it has been, but for the Romans it proved no barrier with the main road from Lincoln to York traversing the river close to the modern day Winteringham (Ad Abum) on the south bank and Brough (Petuaria) on the north bank. The crossing from Winteringham is recorded as being between Tranymere Corner and Flashmire. There has been speculation as to whether there was a ferry across the river or whether the Hum-

ber in early days was shallow enough to be walked across on foot, a feat tested by Lord Noel Buxton in 1953 when he walked across the river in 1953, from a point between Winteringham and Whitton. Later attempts have also been made, including one by 6ft 9in tall businessman, Graham Boanas, of Swanland, Hull, who took four hours to get across the

Boat excavations at North Ferriby.

Above: Triumphant Lord Noel Buxton. Below: Graham Boanas battles through cloying mud.

river with a window of just 30 minutes to get across some of the lowest normally submerged sandbanks. He followed a route from Brough, across to the island of Whitton Sand and then to Whitton. He reportedly said: "It was the most tiring thing I have ever done, but I enjoyed it."

What is beyond doubt from archaeological finds is the presence of Romans in Winteringham, from which the only realistic purpose would appear to be crossing the river itself.

The Chalybeate spring, close to the foot of the Wolds, and the proximity of the fresh water near to the passage to the sea is said to be another attractive proposition for the Romans being at Winteringham.

As the Roman Empire receded there came the Anglo-Saxons, originally invited for payment to help protect the lands of the Celtic king Vortigern from the Picts and Scots. The Angles came from a part of Angulus in Schleswig near the modern day German border with Denmark while the neighbouring Saxons came from the coastal area between the Rivers Elbe and Weser.

As money for payments ran out the foreign guests simply took land and their settlement encouraged more from back home to head for these shores, along with Jutes from modern day Denmark. Being seafaring people the areas around the Humber proved attractive places to settle.

Masted Baltic bound vessels were once a common sight on the Trent, Humber and Ouse.

Following on from the Anglo-Saxons there were Viking raids from the late eighth century involving what would have been modern day Danes, Swedes and Norwegians.

The raids intensified in the 9th century and by 876, York had become the capital of a new Viking Kingdom, with the Ouse and Humber Estuary a vital international routeway for the Vikings, who lost control of York in 954, but continued vicious attacks on modern day Britain, extorting money or Danegeld.

In due course many chose to settle rather than raid and their legacy is in many place names around the Humber, though there were still incursions with the Anglo-Saxon Chronicle recording that in 1013, the then king of Denmark, Swein Forkbeard, had sailed along the Humber and up the River Trent as far as Gainsborough.

The Humber has links with probably the most notable battle of our home shores, the Battle of Hastings. The Kent down is somewhat distant from the Humber Estuary but it was the routeway for the Scandinavian King Harold Hardrada and his men who were defeated by the English king Harold God-winson at the Battle of Stamford Bridge near York. The embattled English king then made his way south to Hastings where he suffered defeat to throne claimant William the Conqueror of Normandy who brought a French influence to England and its system of administration.

The swamplands which beset the upper reaches of the Humber and the valleys of inflowing rivers has already been mentioned and it is worth noting the works which helped produce the 'sea bed' landscapes of today.

The most dramatic of the drainage works were in the Isle of Axholme where the flow of a sizeable meandering river was diverted in two directions to enable land to be reclaimed from the marshes.

The River Don was traditionally the dividing line between the old West Riding of Yorkshire and the Lindsey area of Lincolnshire. The geographical significance notable as it remains as a line dividing the Archbishoprics of York and Canterbury.

Today the main channel of the river heads northwards to feed into the 'Dutch River near Goole while other waters are channelled into the River Trent down river of the King George V road and rail bridge at Keadby.

Much of the old riverbed of the River Don is now built on but evidence of its past influence still persists in local communities.

In Eastoft, north of the township of Crowle, there remains a pub called the River Don Tavern and one side of the road heading north to south retains the name Yorkshireside.

A number of buildings in the area are named in memory of Cornelius Vermuyden, the Dutch engineer charged with the task of diverting the River Don and draining Hatfield Chase and surrounding lands in 1626.

His work was not universally applauded because of the impact on the local economy of those who depended on the marshes and meandering rivers for their livelihoods.

Vermuyden set up base on a river island at Sandtoft in 1626 and claimed to have finished his work in the area in 1630, though many of the settlers remained.

By 1642 there was a slackening of law and order with the English Civil War and a foreigners settlement at Sandtoft, boasting 200 houses, was attacked by local residents unhappy with the drainage works. The then settlement at Sandtoft was finally razed to the ground in 1688.

At the time Sandtoft boasted a population of around 1,000 made up of Dutch, French, Flemish and Belgians who had move to the area to work on the drainage of the Isle of Axholme and Hatfield and Thorne wastes.

The conflict between the drainage engineers and the local communities is touched on in a local history, obliquely called The Manuscript in a Red Box, on account of it being left anonymously at a publisher in a red box. The manuscript is thought to have been written by a Crowle clergyman.

Details of the Don's diversion were recalled in the studies of Dr Philip Ireson a clergyman once based at Eastoft, who in his work, On the Trail of the Old River Don, noted: "The first effect was flooding. Vermuyden seriously underestimated the amount of water flowing along the Don and disastrous floods swamped the area when the Keadby channel proved inadequate."

Dr Ireson wrote: "As the Don silted up, the drainage systems which had relied on it for centuries also broke down."

He also noted villages, although being drained of water were being made something of a backwater.

"The Don villages lost their direct river links with the outside world. It was a tortuous and dangerous journey by land to York or Selby, but by boat and with favourable tides it was possible to reach the northern capital within a day."

Adlingfleet on the River Don, close to its confluence with the Trent, and the Trent's confluence with the River Ouse, had long been a significant trading settlement and a place for stopping off on the way up the Humber or Trent. Significantly today it boasts one of England's oldest stone buildings - a barn.

Dr Ireson notes it is hard to imagine the villages that remain along the route of the Old River Don as once being seafaring communities.

Moving downstream from Eastoft we find Luddington on the Lincolnshire side and Haldenby on the Yorkshire side, the twin communities of Garthorpe on the Lincolnshire side and Fockerby in the West Riding, before Adlingfleet, the last settlement downstream.

Dr Ireson pointed out that a medieval record of 1370 noted the murder of a Luddington sailor on a boat on the River Ouse. He also mentioned an act of piracy.

The Rev Stonehouse in his History of the Isle of Axholme notes villagers were initially worse off : "After Cornelius Vermuyden had diverted the course of the River Idle, stopped the southern branch of the River Don and left the country through which these navigable rivers formerly passed, imperfectly drained, being fenny and moorish and full of carrs, the Isle became more inaccessible from Yorkshire and Nottinghamshire than it was in former times when boats went from Haxey to Finningley, and Westwood-

side to Bearswood Green, Thorne. The ancient communication between
Doncaster and the Trent was cut off by Vermuyden's operations."

The community of Owston Ferry served as the port for the Isle of Axholme, through which goods were imported and exported.

The River Ancholme, rises at Spridlington, to the north east of Lincoln
and joins the River Humber at South Ferriby. Like the area of the Isle of
Axholme prior to drainage works it was a marshland valley with the name
'carrs' being indicative of its low lying topography.

Details relating to the drainage were featured in a dissertation by Professor Allan Shaw of Exeter. Initial works, with the help of Dutchmen, were
carried out by Sir John Monson from 1635 to 1639, though the need for
work to be carried out had long been recognised.

Professor Shaw noted: "The earliest reference to the conditions of the
levels was in 1288, when Edward I, directed a writ of Ad Quod Dampnum
to the shireeve of the county to enquire whether it would be hurting to him
or any other if the course of the water, then obstructed from a place called
Bishop's Brigg (off the A46) to the River Humber were opened so that the
current of the same might be reduced to its due and ancient channel."

From Roman times the valley was not permanently flooded because
there is evidence of tiles and pottery being made at South Ferriby.

"Roman settlement however kept either to Ermine Street (a Roman Road
from Lincoln) to the west or to Middlegate (an old routeway) on the chalk
to the east. Spring tides in the Humber were sufficiently high to prohibit
any outflow of water, so freshwater floods were frequent in the middle part
of the valley."

The Ancholme valley has but a very gentle incline, the river dropping
just 20ft in its final 30 miles. It also presented the added problem of the

The old Hope and Anchor at Ferriby Sluice.

The bridge at Horkstow: Humber Yawl Club archive.

River Humber being above the level of the River Ancholme for many hours each day, thereby not allowing an outflow of water. Even today the tidal Humber restricts outflow from the valley but a properly built sluice system at South Ferriby reduces the threat of flooding.

Sir John Monson's work included a new cut for the River Ancholme from Bishop's Bridge to Horkstow and the construction of a sluice, using stone from Thornton Abbey, at South Ferriby.

In 1767 an Act of Parliament relating specifically to the Ancholme Drainage was passed and a new sluice and lock were built just to the north of the present one.

John Rennie, submitted a report to the Commission in 1800 and a second Act of Parliament was passed in 1802 with various improvement works being completed through to 1844.

While today Brigg may seem to be simply a haunt for pleasure boats, in years gone by the river cut and drainage works enabled it to be an active part of the riverside communities feeding into the River Humber with a steam packet service running from Bishopbridge and sloops and keels carrying a variety of goods upriver to Brigg, which once exported rabbit furs to China, and downriver fertilisers, grain and wool.

Today the main attraction in the upper Ancholme is a Cider Centre at Brandy Wharf, boasting several types of cider, a nearby campsite and a recently installed slipway. Further upstream is the river's now renovated second lock at Harlam Hill.

Many of the bridges along the Ancholme are listed constructions but standing above them all is the iron suspension bridge at Horkstow, which was designed by Sir John Rennie and dates back to 1835/36. At one end is the Wolds village of Horkstow where tessellated Roman mosaics have been unearthed, while the other bank was once the home of one of the area's local brickyards, bricks and tiles being a staple cargo for keels and sloops.

The picturesque bridge has a span of 133ft 9ins with a 14ft roadway, still crossable today, though all that remains on the westward side is a rough track hugging the river and winding towards Winterton. The road decking is supported by iron chains feeding from two stone towers. Remedial work was carried out to the bridge in the 1990s.

Prior to the building of the bridge there was a toll ferry across the Ancholme roughly where the bridge is today.

The lock and sluice at South Ferriby is a scheduled monument.

An indication of the contrasting waters of the canalised Ancholme and the tidal River Humber is given in an Environment Agency advice leaflet.

It says: "The Humber Estuary is characterised by strong currents and shifting mud banks and shoals, so craft navigating the estuary should ensure they are well equipped and have a competent master in charge."

The mainly pleasure craft, on the Ancholme are advised to contact the harbour authorities before venturing on to the River Humber.

Marshlands on either side of the River Humber have been reclaimed and sandbanks in the river have also emerged from the depths.

Those working within the river relate tales of how the main channel is forever changing as silt and debris is deposited, both from the coast and from erosion of hillsides and valleys well inland.

At low tide many of the sandbanks are visible but it is not surprising for yachtsmen, or in the older days, for the ferries between Hull and New Holland, to find themselves stranded on a sandbank.

Because of the preponderance of sandbanks in the river many of the vessels using it were designed with flat bottoms so if they grounded they would simply have to wait for the next tide to float them off. Landing on the sand was fairly common, especially for maintenance work.

Many sloops also landed on sandbanks to enable them to load up with a cargo of sand for the building trade.

The curiously named Sunk Island on the north bank was gradually reclaimed from the sea, as was the once inhabited Read's Island on the south bank, which in recent years has been severed in half by the tides and with the loss of fresh water has been abandoned to the birds.

Like the Isle of Axholme, Sunk Island engenders the feeling one is driving along a one-time sea bed akin to those in the Dutch polderlands.

But the land is famed for being very much England and has a claim to fame as Yorkshire's fourth Riding, though as most in the area know, the

Read's Island at dusk

Riding is derived from a third, so there could not be a fourth Riding to accompany the North, West and East Ridings. Nonetheless in the realm of fiction Sunk Island is author Winifred Holtby's South Riding and Cold Harbour Colony.

The sandbar on which Sunk Island was built emerged from the Humber in 1560 and was for a long time known as Sonke Sands. The land had emerged from the sea and thereby became part of the Crown's lands and in 1668 was leased to Col Anthony Gilbey, who began further reclaiming it from the estuary.

The island became linked to the mainland with a series of roads from the 1840s and its inlet at Stone Creek became an established port with staithes, a weighbridge and its own harbourmaster. The creek's name was due to the importation of stone through the inlet for various churches in Holderness.

Read's Island, close to the south bank of the river off South Ferriby, boasted a house up until the early 1990s and memories of life there are featured elsewhere in this book.

Many expect the island to be 'Reeds Island' reflecting vegetation along the margins of the estuary, however, its name stems not from the plant but the farmers from Burton-upon-Stather who reclaimed the land.

Others give it a somewhat more romantic name culled from a verse by Lincolnshire Poet Alfred Lord Tennyson, who wrote:

On either side of the River lie
Long fields of Barley and of Rye

That Clothe the World and Meet the Sky;
And thro' the field the road runs by
To many towered Camelot,
And up and down the people go,
Gazing where the lilies blow
Round and island there below
The island of Shallott.

Local historian Raymond Carey, a retired fire officer, wrote of the possible association in a history of Read's Island published in The River and John Frank, in aid of the Humber Keel and Sloop Preservation Society and the churches of South Ferriby and Horkstow in 1997.

It seems quite possible Tennyson, whose family owned land in the Grimsby/Cleethorpes area, saw the island, easily viewable from an historic Wolds road, Middlegate, which traversed northwards from Caistor. However, the poet would have had to have used his imagination and waxed lyrical for his poem was published in 1832, when the sandbank was still emerging from the river. It was first referred to as Read's Island in 1851.

Mr Carey points out that in Roman times the river bank extended more than 600 metres out into the Humber so today's island may once have been part of the mainland, being scoured away over the centuries prior to it being reclaimed in subsequent years.

He notes that what today is known as Read's Island in navigation maps of 1734 was noted as being Ferriby Sand or Old Warp. It has been suggested the loss of a French vessel resulted in silt building up behind it but Mr Carey speculates changes in the outfall from the Ancholme and elsewhere in the river may have also contributed.

The end result was that by 1820 vegetation was readily growing on the mudbank and the emerging mass was acquired by the Read brothers of Burton, who further reclaimed it from the river by regular warping, which enables high tide water to be trapped behind barriers like walls and slowly drained back to the sea, in the course of which silt and mud is added to the landmass, rather than it being sucked away by the tides. By 1836 the initial warping had produced an embanked island of 40 acres, which was increased to 80 acres by 1841 and to 400 acres by the 1900s.

The use of the island for active farming and shooting created a reason for maintaining defences but this gradually became less economic and in 1987 the island's defences were seriously breached. Today it is a bird sanctuary, famed as a breeding area for avocets, a species quite rare on these shores.

Chapter 5: Linking Communities

The jetty at Blacktoft, which is used by vessels as a lay-by between tides.

NOWADAYS it is hard to imagine the Humber, Trent, Ouse and tributaries as the main means of communication, not only from village to village or small town, to city but in the days of stage coaches and before the railways it was the most reliable route to the capital.

There were packet boats a plenty heading up both the Trent and the Ouse, connecting small communities with the port of Hull and giving coastal access to the north and to London down south, and transhipment across the continent.

The estuary had wide open stretches but it was the remote narrow inlets which attracted smugglers, with the movement of illicit Dutch gin giving the south bank railway town of New Holland its name.

Through the ages the tidal estuary was the source of much skulduggery with Viking raids, acts of piracy and the smuggling of goods through inlets and small wharfs into the 21st Century.

In a local history, Trail of the Old River Don, clergyman Philip Ireson notes a sinister event on the old River Don, close its mouth into the Trent and the latter's confluence with the Ouse to form the Humber.

"Extraordinary tales of inland piracy emerge from 1271, when Walter de Useflet and others are charged with seizing the Abbott of Selby's ships, in the common passages of Don at Ludynton, Gerlethorp, Haldenby and Folcardeby and carrying off goods and chattels of the Abbott and his men to

The light on the trailing wall at the confluence of the Trent (to the left) and the Ouse (ahead and left, with Blacktoft jetty in the background. This is where the Humber is born.

the value of 20 marks.

Incidences of smuggling around the river Humber and its tributaries were rife with liquor and tobacco, but some of the goods, like tea, were not what we might normally consider to be contraband.

Archives at Gainsborough Library reveal that even in the 1890s there was quite a bit of dealing in smuggled goods.

"The Ship Tavern by the Baltic Oil Mill, in Bridge Street, was a pub notorious for its illegal activities."

A long flight of steps from the back door of the tavern led down to the water's edge, making it easy to unload shipments of contraband brought from the Humber ports under the cover of darkness.

"One story tells of the day that Tom Trevethick's shipyard had a close shave with the law when on his way to obtain cigars, smuggled in from Holland, he saw in the distance, the smuggler he was to meet, accompanied by two policemen. Tom soon forgot about his cigars."

Trevethick's shipyard and wharf was close to the town's Trent Bridge, a toll bridge which was approved in 1787 at a cost of £1,200. Tolls were abolished in 1930.

In his book, Smuggling in Yorkshire 1700-1850, Graham Smith rightly identifies the amount of smuggling which takes place as being directly related to the tax differentials between the country it comes from and the one it goes to.

While tobacco and liquor have high differentials today, in the past tea was a lucrative cargo for smugglers, with a startling three times as much illegal tea coming into the country in 1750, than legal tea. However, William Pitt, virtually ended the tea smuggling in 1784, when he slashed duty from 125 per cent to 12.5 per cent.

Gin and tobacco were smuggled from Holland, Belgium, Germany and America.

Mr Smith records that excise officers often seized smuggled goods as far inland as Leeds, Sheffield, Doncaster and Retford.

The maritime influence on communities inland is noted in a history of Selby by Patricia Scott. The influence continued into the 1990s with tugs, ferries and fishing boats being built on the Ouse at Cochrane's Shipyard.

She notes a shipyard was established in the town's Ousegate by John Foster in the 1750s.

"All kinds of business connected with shipping sprang up, including rope and sail making and iron founding. The shops did a roaring trade provisioning the vessels and clothing the crews."

She notes that from a population of 4,097 in 1821, those linked to shipping included: watermen and their families 830; carpenters and families 134; ropers etc, 100; blockmakers, 60; sailmakers, 50; and labourers and their families 160.

Returning to smuggling, Mr Smith records that a senior exchequer offi-

The tidal bore on the River Trent provided problems for unprepared sailors. Channelling of the river now means such waves riding inland are rarely as big as the one featured above.

The busy port of Gainsborough was also a centre of activity for smugglers.

cial was sent to Hull in 1417 to investigate smuggling. He found both York and Beverley were shipping wool to Holland "without custom", with any small harbour or creek being used to escape duty.

Sloops were deployed along the coast and in the river in an attempt to reduce smuggling but with limited resources and the scale of the problem it was too much for them kill it off.

Mr Smith, a former librarian and archivist for Her Majesty's Customs and Excise, notes that in 1745, Captain Joseph Cockburn, a poacher turned gamekeeper, who was in charge of a customs cutter, recalled in his past life that the master of a York keel had obtained legal permits for half ankers of brandy which were taken up to Gainsborough on the keel, where they were landed legally as if they had been brought down from York duty paid. An anker was a Dutch cask containing 10.25 gallons of liquor.

In the 1770s the customs officers were noted as having the assistance of 21 dragoons with 10 at Patrington, seven at Hedon and four at Aldborough. In 1846, 15 tons of tobacco was seized in Hull and 250 persons convicted while in 1851 a £10 reward was offered in the hunt for the master of the sloop Samuel and Susannah of Goole, who following alleged smuggling, had had his vessel condemned in the Exchequer Court.

Smuggling was not simply a way for a single vessel owner, or sailor, to make a bit on the side, but was done on an industrial basis with gin distilleries on the continent banking on the English trade, up to the First World War, when large Dutch vessels followed the fishing fleets of East Coast ports supplying them with duty free goods.

The head of the Humber prior to 1930s, when a training wall was built along the main channels, was a mile wide expanse of water at the confluence of the Ouse and Trent, with the shallows known as Blacktoft Sands, curiously now on the south bank while the village is on the north bank. It can cause confusion for people visiting the RSPB nature reserve on the south of the Ouse where sandbanks have become permanent land due to warping. Up until the 1930s the main channel up the Ouse moved between Blacktoft and Adlingfleet.

People owning land along the river banks were obliged to provide wood to maintain the banks and staithes, of which there were three at Blacktoft.

A vessel called the Clement, which sailed out of Blacktoft in 1471, is recorded in a village history as exporting 42 stone of wool and 2,307 sheep-skins to France via Hull, returning with 2,000 gallons of wine. In 1511, 23 chauldrons of coal were brought to Blacktoft by the Bartholomew from Newcastle. A chauldron was a unit of dry capacity used for measuring coal relating to wagon size and at this time a Newcastle chauldron would have been between 42 and 52 hundredweight. Coal was taxed by the chauldron and not by weight, thus it was to one's advantage to use larger chauldrons.

While a port in the past, Blacktoft today remains strategically placed as a safe resting berth for vessels between tides, ensuring they have enough depth in the river to make it to their destination.

The Aire and Calder Navigation Company added a £5,500 wooden jetty which was used by packet boats to transport both cargo and passengers travelling to Selby, Goole, Thorne and Hull. A new concrete jetty was opened in 1956 and the small community boasted a customs official up to 1967. Probably its most famous moment was in a wartime German propa-

A steam packet at the jetty in Burton Stather, below the twin village of Burton-upon-Stather.

ganda broadcast by Lord Haw-Haw, who reported Blacktoft Docks had been bombed.

With few bridges across rivers, communities relied on small ferries to traverse local rivers. Just like the bridges there was usually a toll for the small vessel service which saw cattle, sheep, cyclists and horseless carriages crossing the water. Some of the ferries were

The steam packet Scarborough en route for the Humber along the Trent, packed with people.

small rowing boat affairs while others were designed for larger cargoes, the last of which was the rail linked ferry service from New Holland to Hull, which came to an end in 1981 with the opening of the Humber Bridge, to be featured in more detail later.

Names like Boothferry on the River Ouse, which gave its name to a local

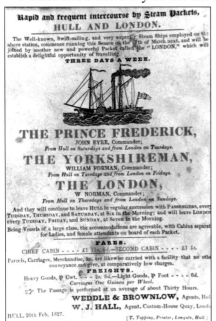

A poster advertising steam packet services from the Humber to London in 1827.

authority area surrounding Goole from 1974 to 1996, and East Ferry on the Trent hark back to the days of river crossings which linked to the steam packet services running from Selby to the Humber and Gainsborough to Hull with further services allowing passengers to travel down to London, other than on horseback or by carriage on less than smooth turnpike roads.

The first steam packets in the guise of the paddle sloop Caledonia, made an appearance around 1814, sailing from Gainsborough to Hull and cutting sailing times to five hours compared with the previous three to four days by sail.

Ferries existed before the coming of the railways and more impor-

A steam packet on the Humber at South Ferriby. Steam packets also travelled down the River Ancholme from Bishopbridge, through the market town of Brigg, to the Humber.

tantly the building of bridges to allow for the development of an extensive road network.

The building of the King George V road and railway bridge at Keadby on the Trent, (opened in 1916) gradually put paid to the King's Ferry across the river at Burton Stather, which lasted into the late 1920s, many others having gone earlier due to the undermining of their income. The Trent ferries and the experiences of the Burton ferryman, typical of many along the rivers, is featured later.

The use of the Trent and Humber as a means of transport is further emphasised by it being one of the routes for pilgrims fleeing northern Lincolnshire, via Killingholme, the site of huge river installations today. The pilgrims were seeking a new life in America but from the Humber headed to Holland, a country which was more tolerant of differing religious views. Some of the pilgrims are known to have set sail from Gainsborough, which in addition to its outstanding medieval hall also has literary roots as the set-

ting for George Elliot's classic novel, Mill on the Floss and links with the Viking kings Sweyne and Canute with the Anglo-Saxon Chronicle noting the former had sailed up the mouth of the Humber and along the Trent to Gainsborough in 1018, the year Canute was chosen as king.

Keels on the River Humber

Gainsborough was a

thorough going maritime community at one time boasting seven ropewalks, one owned by the Bourn family continuing into the 1890s. Three sail makers were noted in the 19th century and there was also shipbuilding in the town with J and H Smith (later Henry Smith), R and W Furley and William Moody. Ships up to 700 tons were built in the yards as well as sloops, brigs and small sailing vessels.

Steam packets ran in the 19th century to Burringham, Doncaster and Hull. The last regular steamer service is thought to be Celia, which continued to run on market days up until the First World War.

Although today most of the industrial wharfs have given way to housing, Gainsborough was a key port of yesteryear with Baltic bound barques sloops and keels heading upstream to Nottingham and beyond and downstream to the Humber and Hull.

The Trent provided access to canals at Stockwith and at Keadby with the Stainforth to Keadby Canal, authorised by an Act of Parliament in 1793, providing access to the coalfields and markets of Sheffield and South Yorkshire. Indeed many of the later sloops and keels were known as 'Sheffield Class' vessels which meant they were of a size to pass through the locks heading down to Sheffield.

Coal itself was one of the major cargoes but there were many others passing along the waterways including chemicals from Howdendyke on the Ouse and bricks and tiles from a variety of brickyards along the River

Coal sidings on the Stainforth to Keadby Canal, at Keadby, showing wagons ready to offload coal into river vessels, via a special coal chute on the banks of the Trent, beyond the distant lock. The canal was often called the Sheffield and South Yorkshire Canal, because it enabled passage along the waterways network to Sheffield.

The specially designed coal chute on the banks of the River Trent at Keadby. Photo courtesy of Bryan Longbone collection.

Humber and particularly in the Barton-upon-Humber area where the former brickyard ponds are used for leisure activities and reputedly protected the community during the 1953 East Coast Floods, with excess waters being absorbed by the old workings.

In the days of containerisation it is easy to forget that even in the 1950s, 1960s and 1970s much cargo was loaded and unloaded from sea going vessels in a labour intensive manner with cranes and slings.

In the 19th and early 20th century ports like Hull were key centres in the transhipment of goods with cargoes being offloaded on to smaller vessels like sloops and keels in Hull, for passage further inland.

The trick for many boatmen was to take a cargo inland from Hull and to find a suitable cargo for the return journey. For example imported barley from South America would be taken from Hull to the mining city of Wakefield, making coal an obvious return cargo.

Other crop cargoes included wheat, maize, linseed, grass, potatoes and sugar beet.

Slag from Scunthorpe steelworks was bagged up and loaded on to vessels at Keadby for shipment to Hull and beyond for use as an agricultural fertiliser. The work in the early days was done by a method of barrows and planking with the vessel gradually moving away from the bank as its load increased. In later years Keadby was better known for its coal chute, which

Heavily laden Sulpho at Stockwith on the River Trent. She sailed with cargoes of chemical fertilisers from Howdendyke which lies on the River Ouse above Goole. Anderton's Chemical Factory had a fleet of such vessels including Sulpho, Hydro, Nitro and Phospho which took cargoes as far as the Wash returning with various cargoes. They took phosphates, pyrites and potash to Howdendyke from Hull. The photo shows skipper Wheldrake midships with his wife to the rear of the vessel and son to the fore. Although sea going she was without bulwarks, presumably to make loading and livering easier. Laden as she is in the photo the lee deck would be awash when sailing but the sparring deck between the two holds would give a dryish area for working the sail winches and bowline and jib sheets. Sulpho is cutter rigged with a bowsprit and jib sails. The boom is over the after deck to give sail area to balance the jib. Skipper Wheldrake, although thought to be illiterate, was on the vessel for around 40 years. The Humber Keel and Sloop Preservation Society Vessel Amy Howson, carried Phosphorous, known as 'fossit' from Hull to Howdendyke.

Vessels heading inland and upstream, had the option to lower their masts to pass under low bridges, though this toll bridge at Selby was capable of opening. Most of the traffic on this section of the River Ouse was heading to the British Oil and Cake Mills at nearby Barlby. Until tolls were abolished the bridge was known for creating long tail backs of traffic.

loaded the fuel, brought by rail from the West Riding, into vessels at the wharf by the entrance to the canal.

Palm kernels and other feedstuffs like fish meal, the former still used to make cattle cake at the British Oil and Cake Mills, Selby were delivered by sloops and keels and barges as opposed to the modern day coaster.

Vessels from Hull also took cocoa products up the Ouse to York, where the Yorkshire Evening Press had its reels of newsprint shipped to its printing centre on the Ouse. The paper moved from its Coney Street premises in 1989 to a site by the city's River Foss, with paper continuing to be delivered by water, to feed the paper's new press, for some time thereafter.

Transportation of fertilisers was quite common, with works at Beverley on the River Hull, Barton on the River Humber and Brigg on the River Ancholme providing deliveries to villages around the area while a fertiliser works at Howdendyke regularly delivered up the River Trent on vessels like the Billy Boy Sulpho for chemical works at Misterton.

Cargoes included copper ore and steel wiring, tinned fruit, dried fruit from South Africa and cargoes of flour and sugar for shipping inland.

In addition to bricks, other building materials included sand, gravel, cement, limestone, potash and timber.

There were several ferries along the rivers Trent, Ouse and Humber, including South Ferriby and North Ferriby, Barton and Hessle, Barton and Hull, New Holland and Hull, Barrow and Hull, Goxhill and Hull, Whitton and Brough and Winteringham and Brough, while on the Trent there was

Many a vessel owner will have enjoyed a convivial pint or more at the Friendship Inn, at Keadby. The top photo was clearly taken well before 1952 when three 'cricket wicket' towers of a coal fuelled power station would have been evident. The station was officially opened in 1955 and closed in 1984, with the towers blown up in 1991. It has now been replaced by a combined cycle gas plant which began generating in 1996. The photo, right, courtesy of Bryan Longbone, shows the 'wicket chimney' of the power station.

East Stockwith and West Stockwith, East Butterwick and West Butterwick, Burringham and Althorpe and Owston Ferry (Kinnard's Ferry) and East Ferry.

An insight into the life of a ferry family is given by Winn Readhead of Burton Stather, which in addition to the aforementioned shipbuilders, also boasted Franks' brickyard.

The village dates back to the Middle Ages ages, when it was granted a market charter and was on a major routeway heading south from Yorkshire into Lincolnshire along the King's Causeway over the Marshlands near Goole and the northern end of the Isle of Axholme, linking by the King's Ferry from Garthorpe on the west bank of the River Trent, to Burton Stather in the east.

By the early 20th century the ferry was licensed by the Board of Trade to the landlord of the Ferry House Inn and was operated through to around 1930 by three members of the Readhead family.

Winn Readhead, son of the last ferryman, Rowland Winn Readhead, and a member of the Burton-upon-Stather Local History Association, related his childhood memories of his father and tales passed down about the ferry and life in a riverside community.

According to Winn his grandfather, also called Winn Readhead, was born in 1879 and came to Burton as a millstone dresser in 1903, most probably to work at the Burton Mill which stood at the bottom of The Avenue in the appropriately named Mill Field.

He had moved into a cottage across the green at Burton Stather from the Ferry House Inn, which originally fronted on to the River Trent and boasted

Ferryman Winn Readhead, senior.

The last ferryman, Rowland Winn Readhead.

The riverside at Burton Stather, with the picnic spot of Burton Hills in the background.

a jetty into the river. A new pleasure craft jetty has recently been added, re-capturing a touch of the village's past.

Winn believes the mill dressing work was limited and consequently his grandfather sought other means of earning cash. Living close to the pub, he took the opportunity of becoming the ferryman when it arose.

"The landlord provided the facilities and was licensed by the Board of Trade. He paid my father and grandfather and provided them with a lunch as part of the payment," he said.

His grandfather operated the ferry from around 1905 through to 1915 when he went into the Royal Artillery and fought in the First World War.

"My father, Rowland Winn Readhead, who was born in 1900 took over, very simply because there was no-one else."

Winn Readhead senior, who fought on the Somme and received the Military Medal, also served as a corporal in India before returning home in 1920.

His son Rowland Winn Readhead went into the navy in 1918 for a couple of years and his brother Osbourne took over the ferry until his father came back. Osbourne then went into service in Nottingham.

Winn junior said it was believed the ferry operated up until 1930, but as with other ferries, it was hit by the opening of the King George V road and rail bridge at Keadby and the subsequent increase in road traffic.

Even after the ferry ceased to operate Rowland Winn Readhead retained the ferry boat and used it on the river for fishing.

"After about 1930 my dad went on the river boats and worked on petrol tankers. Burton Stather was a petrol depot up to 1939/40. Petrol came in by tanker from Hull and was of-floaded and then reloaded into smaller tankers which went up river to Nottingham, Gainsborough and wherever."

Winn said there was a fleet of craft which operated from Burton, which he believes included Energie, Fidelitie, Alacritie all with an 'ie' at the end rather than a 'y'.

Winn recalled the ferry boat as being a working boat and not a gaily painted pleasure craft. It was a dull bluish grey colour and had no name.

"It was like a heavy rowing boat, the local name is a 'coggie', you could get nine or 10 people in there with their bikes as well."

Those with bikes were not

The Ferry at Burringham. The crossing was from the Ferryboat pub which became Take a Gander.

just local people heading for the steelworks at Scunthorpe but included cyclists from Yorkshire using the ferry en route to Cleethorpes.

All manner of materials were carried on the boat including livestock, bricks, tiles and drainage pipes, mineral water, farm produce. The farm produce headed eastwards from the fertile lands of the north of the Isle of Axholme while the bricks and tiles of the Franks family yard at Burton Stather headed westwards on the ferry for local building projects. For moving bricks and tiles further afield the Frank family had a fleet of sloops.

Burton historian, Geoff Robinson in a parish history, refers to the shipyard, mentioned earlier, which in addition to the sailing ship Burton Stather, built 341 vessels including fishing smacks and colliers.

Winn Readhead junior believes the ferry in its latter days cost 9d but from his elder brothers and mother Annie, was told tales of his father returning home with potatoes and on one occasion a chicken, which he had accepted as payment for the crossing.

The ferry boat was not rowed across the river but was sculled across by his father, who would be stood at the rear of the craft operating one oar from the stern.

With the pull of incoming and outgoing tides, the path across the river was not in a straight line, with the boat being sculled on an arc-shaped course to take account of which way the tide was running.

Winn recalled the old ferry boat being hauled up on land on occasions to be recaulked, which sealed any gaps between the wooden planking of the boat. The bottom of the boat would be given a coating of tar.

Winn was brought up in two sets of semi-detached homes called Trent View, his former home now number 122, Stather Road. The location of the houses was a touch above the seasonal flood level which regularly affected properties in riverside communities prior to the building of major flood defence mounds along the river bank.

The ferry was to some degree seasonal, with fewer people crossing in the winter. His father was able to find work digging clay at the brickyard, where clay was dug out in the winter and piled up ready for making bricks in the summer.

The ferry operated from the Ferry House Inn on the east bank but if anyone wanted to be rowed across they would ring a bell outside Webb's Hotel, which stood on the western bank of the Trent. Winn can recall seeing the hotel as a young boy but by then it had been boarded up.

In the days before the war the River Trent was known for its salmon and Winn's father Rowland Winn Readhead, villager Bill Bull and 'Cap' Day were all licensed to fish for salmon under the 1923 Salmon and Freshwater Fisheries Act 1923, by the Board of Conservators for the Trent Fishery District.The license allowed them to fish for salmon and in Bill Bull's case with a 'topping net'.

Winn recalled his father catching salmon and selling them to local hostelries like the Sheffield Arms, the Flixborough Inn and in earlier days to the Webb's Hotel at Garthorpe.

He recalled on one occasion his father returned home with a 40lb salmon and was always unhappy with a display at Scunthorpe museum which noted a salmon of lesser size as the biggest caught in the Trent.

In those days household freezers were essentially a thing of the future and consequently the fish was sold or eaten quickly before

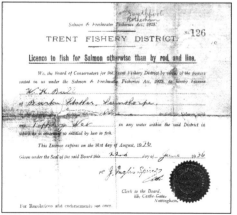

William Bull's salmon fishing certificate.

it went off.

Local people also caught dab-like flat fish in the river by hook and line but the most commonly caught fish was the eel.

The eels were mainly caught by a method called 'blobbing' where a conical device with dangling threads of wool was put in the river overnight. The fish, thinking the threads were food, would seek to eat them and in the process their teeth would become entangled in the threads. Winn recalled they would haul in five or six eels from one blob. He said people would collect their eels in the morning and then have them for breakfast.

The river eels had extra sharp teeth and having caught one by hook and line

George Exton with a gigantic salmon.

on one occasion Winn recalled taking out the hook and the painful experience of the fish then latching on to his finger and almost biting off the end.

"My father caught the grandfather of all eels. It was a conger eel and 6ft long. It would not normally be seen in the river but had become stranded in a sandbank pool."

He said his father had killed the eel with an oar. It would have been too dangerous to tackle it any other way.

Winn has memories of his father occupying the spare minutes by splicing pieces of rope and practising knots. He said his father was not very tall but was a powerful man with big arms. In later years he worked as a rigger on the steelworks in Scunthorpe and one of his colleagues recalled him as one of the most effective older riggers he had known.

Salmon were also a feature of the tidal stretches further up the Trent, as demonstrated by a wonderful early photo of a 30lb specimen proudly displayed by George Exton of Owston Ferry, while boatman Goff Sherburn of Goole recalls picking them up from sandbanks at low tides.

George's son Eddie Exton, now of Haxey, recalled his father George fishing for salmon and the family knitting new nets each year.

"This was done yearly because the twine available at that time soon perished. The last thing you wanted to happen was to be dipping out a 20lbs salmon that was thrashing about in the net and for the net to give way, dropping half a week's wages back in the water.

He said that because the river was so laden with silt in the lower reaches the salmon swam on the top where there was more oxygen. Those fishing the river could spot a dorsal fin close to the surface or sticking out.

"Passengers in the ferry boat often had an unplanned excursion and sometimes were left stranded on the wrong side of the river while the ferryman pursued a fish."

The ferry rights at Owston were owned by the landlords of the White Hart, on the banks of the Trent.

The landing of fish on a Sunday was prohibited, but, villagers found ways of secreting them away wired to the underside of vessels to ensure they still benefited from what the Lord had provided.

The ferrymen and passing boats also did some underhand barter trading with a touch of shrinkage or damaged goods in products like butter and sugar, which they exchanged for rabbits, pheasants and the like.

As with Selby, the river linked Owston Ferry with the 'outside world'.

"The village was lined from end to end with jetties, wharves and moorings of different shapes, sizes and designs," said Mr Exton.

At the start of the 20th century the community was still a busy inland port, which saw a gradual decline and said goodbye to its ferry crossing in the early 1950s.

"Owston Ferry was a point of entry from which a lot of the Isle of Axholme imported goods came in. These would include stone, fertiliser, paraffin, coal, grocery and provisions and manufactured goods.

"The port exported farm products which included food, grain, meat on the hoof and flax. It also had a small fishing fleet.

"Boats would be loaded and unloaded, very often by men wheeling the cargo across planks from ship to shore as only a few of the wharves had a crane or derrick. Baskets were produced in the village for the fishing industry and agricultural uses.

"The Gainsborough United Steam Packet Co, which plied the river with its paddle boats, carried almost everything between Hull and Gainsborough, including passengers doing business and shopping trips. This steam packet would stop at a number of places along the river and a return ticket from Gainsborough to Hull in 1909 was 1s 6d (7.5p).

"John Snowdon and Albert Leggot of Owston Ferry also ran market

Vessels on the River Humber, off Winteringham Haven, showing a paddle steamer pulling a train of barge craft. Similar sights were common on the Trent.

boats to Hull and Gainsborough."

He said "cuckoo boats" from on the Chesterfield Canal, would also load and off-load cargoes and navigate downstream to the South Yorkshire Canal.

In the 1920s and 1930s the Trent was not as channelled as it is today and many communities along the river and also the Humber and Ouse would learn to live with seasonal flooding.

Mr Exton, said: "My first recollection of the river was watching the boats go by. When high tides were on I would be lifted over the front door dam board to paddle on the road and pavement, which was flooded."

He said the lower part of the house was tarred to keep out the river water and villagers kept a close eye on the tides. Sand bags were readily available and families anticipated lifting their carpets and sofas above flood levels.

"Suddenly, without any warning the whole street would be suffering from an epidemic of dam board fever. Everyone who had a door, gate or other opening would be putting clay around the sides and bottom, squashing a dam board on to it and then reinforcing it with sandbags," said Mr Exton.

Such precautions, however, were inadequate for many communities in March, 1947, when the Trent river bank gave way at Morton Gap near Gainsborough, resulting in a near 20-mile lake, halted only by dam-boarding the gaps in the Frodingham rail viaduct off Scotter Road, Scunthorpe. Plans had been made to evacuate residents of the town's Lodge Moors estate into a school at the top of the borough's escarpment.

With the advent of steam it became commonplace to see sloops, keels and Thames barges, being given a tow against the tide, or to enable them to catch the tide and ride it either up or down the Humber, a process further outlined in the fact that river traffic had priority and Acts of Parliament had to be sought for the building of bridges and later on the sealing of bridges like Keadby lift road and rail bridge in 1956. The bridge had opened in

It was anything but plain sailing for vessels trapped in the frozen Trent and featured above and below, while to the left one can make out a few figures in the landscape as villagers at Amcotts experienced the delights of walking on water, albeit frozen water.

The frozen river at Owston Ferry, with villagers, probably unwisely venturing out on to the water.

May, 1916, replacing a former rail only bridge a few yards upstream, which had opened to traffic in 1864. The proposed sealing of the more modern bridge met with opposition from the people in Gainsborough because it limited the size of vessels able to pass upriver.

In days gone by there were many boatyards and maritime trades connected with the trade on the rivers, including shipbuilders at Paull, Hessle, Barton and Winteringham, Goxhill and New Holland on the Humber and Owston Ferry and Burton Stather, on the Trent. They were not just small craft but vessels built for sailing to distant lands.

The moving sandbanks of the Humber and the Trent were not the only problem for mariners.

Mr Exton, who grew up in South Street, Owston Ferry, and penned a successful local history book, When I Was Born a Poacher, recalled some bad winters.

"The heavy snowfalls and bitter cold temperatures were creating ice floes on the river. These were formed in outfalls, culverts and large shallow areas at the mouth of the Trent and in the River Humber. Each tide brought more and larger pieces of ice up the river. By the beginning of the third week of January all the river traffic had been brought to a halt and the ferry boats had stopped plying the muddy waters."

Mr Exton reported that on Sunday, January 21, 1940, villagers John Eyer, Herman Fletcher and Noel Grant made a round trip on the ice across the river.

He reported John Eyer recounting the feat: "I ran to within four or five feet of the other bank and the ice gave way. I knew it was shallow there because we would swim there in a summertime, so I only went up to the

Ice-locked vessels at the entrance to the Louth Navigation, by Tetney Lock at the mouth of the River Humber. Photo: Stuart Sizer collection.

The frozen Trent at Gainsborough, provided an opportunity for ice skating.

knees as did Herman behind me."

The feat was repeated by Mr Eyer over the next four days as he was in the habit of taking the ferry boat across the river to link up with a bus service down to Gainsborough where he worked.

There are accounts of people walking across the River Trent lower down the river at Amcotts, but today the river is unlikely to freeze because of power stations upstream and the channelling of the river, which makes it harder for ice to form. Lower downstream the drop of the tide also limits the formation of solid sheets of ice.

The channelling of the water stream also reduces the size of the tidal bore, known as the aegir. While the Humber is less likely to freeze there have been arctic winters with ice sheeting in some areas and heavy ice floes in the shipping lanes.

Another of the trades which came to Althorpe, next to Keadby Bridge, was the processing of Baltic whale oil with a factory established by the Southern Oil Mills, manufacturing margarine. The operation ended in 1957.

Three men and cases of Beltox lard in 1932-3. The lard was made at the Southern Oil Mills on the Althorpe side of Keadby Bridge as seen above. On the left is Len Plumtree and on the right is Herbert Hunter. The factory closed in 1957.

Chapter 6: Skills of Yesteryear

The Barton Regatta Committee from 1929, possibly stood on the side deck of the tug Ace Tut. The man crouched down at the front is Shadrac Goodson, with the others from the left: Tom West, Billie Foster, Arthur Hedley, Tom Hoodless, Nanse Lindley, unknown, Stan Robson and Billie Barraclough. Photo courtesy the Humber Keel and Sloop Preservation Society.

THE ways of riverfolk and their lifestyle are passing into oblivion with even those who worked on barge type craft, into the 1970s, mostly now, like myself, seasoned members of the grey haired wrinkly crew.

Their personal experience and the memories of those who recalled life as far back as the sail era, which effectively came to an end by the Second World War, are noted here, along with knowledge imparted through previously recorded memories.

In addition there are recollections from those with the smaller motorised craft and dumb barges which were quite common as working vessels into the late 1970s and early 1980s.

Goff Sherburn, (when interviewed, aged 79), father of Chris Sherburn, owner of the restored keel Southcliffe, was born in Thorne during the depression of the late 1920s and in the 1930s, moved to Goole, initially to Duckels Buildings in Old Goole and then, Don Street, appropriately by the River Don.

The Duckels buildings were alongside a shipyard, now long gone, as are many, but not all of the seafaring traditions of the once thriving inland port which although seemingly quieter, even today provides berths for sea going vessels.

With a hint of sadness, Goff said: "If I mention any business in Goole it has gone."

He said most of the men in Goole during the war were away on war work or serving in the merchant navy.

"Goole was a very busy port at that time. We had bacon boats, butter boats, coal and steel boats, whatever you care to name."

Another feature was what were known locally as 'Lankys' which were the vessels of the Yorkshire and Lancashire railway, the rail-

A classic image of a couple living on a boat. Photo: HKSPS.

ways being instrumental in the construction of port facilities at Goole.

Youngsters in old Goole were given the opportunity to skip conventional schooling once aged 13, spending their last year at school with some sort of employment, which for Goff was working on the farm of Everatt Oates nine miles down the Swinefleet Road. He cycled there and back each day

Market boatmen at Barton Haven in the 1930s. From the left, the skipper with his dog and his mate, the brothers Windle and three rulleymen who pushed barrows loaded with goods, including on the right G Dent and (second left from him) J Lawtey, from Barrow-upon-Humber.

Sloops in the Barton Regatta of 1929, with the controlling vessel King Tut. Saxby won the race.

and recalled the majority of workers on the farms in those days were German and Italian prisoners of war. He left school altogether aged 14.

Goff then joined a fleet of barges owned by Thomas I Acaster. He did his National Service from 1949 to 1951, returning to Acaster's which ran coal from the Yorkshire collieries to Flixborough Wharf on the River Trent to feed John Lysaght's steelworks on the crest of the escarpment in Scunthorpe above the River Trent, this particular steelworks closing in 1981.

He worked there from 1952 to 1954 and recalled the coal was delivered by dumb barges (engineless vessels) pulled by tugs.

He was then offered a job by the British Transport Corporation (1954 to 1979) working with floating coal-carrying compartment vessels which were towed or pushed by tug as explained in an earlier chapter. He worked there for 25 years, being skipper of the steam tugs Highgate (No 17) and Water-

A busy scene on the canal at Keadby.

Riverside sports on Beverley Beck. Photo: HKSPS.

loo (No 6). He also occasionally worked on other tugs.

The Waterloo was then converted to diesel and subsequently the number of tugs needed on the operation was reduced from 13 to seven tugs with Goff becoming skipper of the Kellingley. The other tugs were also named after Yorkshire collieries.

Goff came out of the trade when a switch was made to carrying smoke-

Competitors taking part in regatta sports at Beverley Beck. The event appears to be a beer barrel coracle style challenge. Photo: HKSPS.

A line of 'Tom Puddings' is pulled along by a tug with a contraption caled a Jebus at the front of the pans cutting through the water like the bows of a boat. The vessel appears to be called Tuon 14.

The coal hoist at Goole, which is due to benefit from restoration work.

less fuel as opposed to the traditional coal. The skippers were paid by the ton and with real coal carried 35 tons as opposed to the 16 tons of smokeless coal, consequently his wages were effectively halved. He said the river work in general, at this point in the late 1970s, was fading away, though he worked for another four years for Effluent Services on barges transferring effluent from Leeds and Doncaster to ships at Goole for disposal in the North Sea.

Goff recalled: "It was never straightforward, supplying coal to Flixborough and anywhere in the Humber or Trent. There was not a man around in those days who did not go aground."

He said the running aground was not through bad management but the frequently changing position of sandbanks, which was evident even today in the River Humber where buoys signalling the shipping channel were moved with some frequency.

Goff said it was so busy with the demand for coal to feed Lysaght's steelworks that the boss of the operation, Edwin Pittwood, would pay anything that floated to carry coal. There were 50 or 60 barges at the time moving coal to Flixborough in the early 1950s.

He said the barges would pull alongside the jetty at Flixborough and the coal would be taken out by gantry cranes with big grabs.

"The Trent was always a difficult river and beyond Keadby it got really bad."

He said the real problem was due to, "the bottom being near the top" and the fact the tides were very rapid.

"In the mid 1940s I can remember there were a couple of vessels still working under sail, which carried all sorts of cargo. The last I remember them doing was going out into the Humber to get river sand. They went down towards Spurn and Cleethorpes."

While sail was on its way out Goff recalls having to learn the old boat-

Sanding was a main occupation of many sloopmen who would land on a sandbank in the river at low tide and then load up with sand before departing on the rising tide. The sand would then be used in the building trade. The Stoney Binks of Spurn was one of the favoured places for sanding. Photo HKSPS.

man's skills of knot tying and splicing.

"You pass things down. When I first started on barges I was 14 and I went to Acaster's. I went with an old lad 'Titch' Whitton. He was a very old boatman then. He was 70 odd and he taught me what he was taught, going back 100 years. I learned splicing and a lot of boating off him."

He said 'Titch' chewed tobacco and would use the same knife to cut his tobacco and cheese and other food without washing it in between.

"He also taught me never to panic. He said there was always a way out."

He said 'Titch' went back to the days when there were no motors to get them out of a hole, so he had other tricks up his sleeve.

Goff also recalled that in the 1940s boatmen like himself were issued with Estuarial Seaman Ration Books, which gave them a seaman's clothing allowance. They also had rights in obtaining provisions.

"If we went up to Hull or Grimsby we could knock up the local policeman, who had to open up the village shop for rations."

He said they also had permits for Grimsby and Immingham docks.

"You did not stop for provisions in tidal waters," he said. "You tried to stick with the tide to get to Goole."

The main reason for not stopping was one would lose the advantage of riding the tide, whether going upstream or downstream.

Goff said the engines fitted to most of the barges were not powerful enough to fight against the tide.

The Middle Whitton lightship helped protect sailors from the treacherous sands.

Villagers taking part in the Keadby Regatta in 1900.

"You did not argue with the tides, you went with them. If you knew you would not get all the way to Goole you tried to get to Blacktoft, which had safe mooring."

He said even today Blacktoft was used as a half-way-house mooring.

In the 1940s, Goff recalled, there were small bantam tugs which often pulled the under-powered barges to help them make progress.

Goff said it was not unusual for one of the coal barges at Flixborough to allow itself to be carried to the confluence with the Ouse, where the skipper would ground the vessel and then hitch a tow back to Goole.

Goff said that in the olden days an anchor was used to halt a vessel but boatmen on dumb barges which had tillers also learned how to manoeuvre by intelligently using the rudder and the anchor.

"On the River Hull, lighter barges would take the vessel down the Hull, riding the tide to the King George Lock basin."

Effectively the basin was like a parking bay with the individual craft waiting to pick up their cargoes.

He said when barges 'dropped down on anchor' at the mouth of the River Ouse others would know what they were doing.

"It was to save you time to get home. There were no radios but people knew what you were doing. You helped each other. You would fall out like hell over a pint at night but you would be okay in the morning."

Goff recalled the days when the Humber, Trent and Ouse were rich with salmon, providing a welcome source of extra income for boatmen.

"I have seen porpoises and there were a lot of salmon in those days. We used to have people buy salmon off us.

He said the two to three feet long salmon were not caught by boatmen fishing for them, but were ones which had foundered on sandbanks while seeking out their spawning grounds.

"They dropped on the sandbanks, we used to get them and there was a potato merchant at Swinefleet who would have them off us."

He said they would 'flog' the salmon for £1, which was a lot of money when wages were £2.50.

Goff said it was a busy river in his early days, with a lot of traffic heading up to the port of Gainsborough, to Newark and on to Nottingham.

"At one time you could see 20 to 30 boats all going up the Trent with different commodities."

He also remembers taking brown sugar up to York and goods up to the basin at Leeds, which was where the Royal Armouries stands. He recalled there was a big petrol basin there.

Living on the boats was a good life with the families on the rivers often called water gypsies.

Along many of the cargo routes were boatmen's missions where the children of boatmen went to school for half a day and which had proper laundry facilities.

This image shows 'blobbing' which had little to do with catching eels, in this case, and more to do with catching and channelling the waters of rivers. Chalk from South Ferriby, was taken to build up the banks of the Trent and Ouse. Photo: HKSPS.

The steam keel Swift, owned by David Holgate and his family, was built at Thorne and is seen here in the Yorkshire town loading 'Prize Medal' beer from Darley's Brewery. One presumes it was not simply for the crew but was being delivered to riverside and canal hostelries. Note the horse dray. Photo courtesy Brian Peeps, HKSPS.

"Families lived on board and you had port health inspectors who came on board the boat and registered how many people you were allowed in the fore cabin and the aft cabin and also what sex."

He said the men generally wore waterproof sealskin trousers or corduroy trousers. They had boatmen's ganzies and traditional bargemen's caps. Women had aprons and shawls.

"You were lucky if you got a man and wife and mate on board, unless the mate was family. If you had a mate they were normally a family member."

He said the husbands and wives would take their turns at whatever needed doing on board, including taking the tiller and cooking the food. The food was mainly stew, which was left bubbling on the stove.

"It was a very close-knit community. If you were not born into it, it was a hell of a job to get into it. It was only just after the war they began breaking the code."

He said a key reason for changes to families living on board was the installation of the 21 horsepower Lister engines. The engines had to go somewhere and either they went in a cabin or the cargo hold. Most went in cabins, otherwise the carrying capacity of the vessel would have been reduced. The knock-on effect was that the vessels could no longer accommodate families.

Lighting in the vessels was by old fashioned paraffin lamps, with a crude wick feeding into a paraffin reservoir. The lighting mechanism was on a

A coal steamer in the higher reaches of Barton Haven with Waterside Road beyond.

gimbal pivot device enabling it to stay level as the vessel dipped and rose in the water. Goff's wife, Eileen, recalls children from 'water gypsy' families attending her school, Old Goole Board School, and having to help teach them.

"They tended to be dressed more old fashioned. When we had shoes they had boots." She said the boat children would have been intelligent in the conventional sense had they had more access to education.

"Those barge children had much more practical skills than the kids in full time school."

Goff recalled one young girl, aged around 15 or 16, from a boat family who could take a Lister engine apart and put it back together again as well as any man.

Thorne-based keel skipper Herbert Rhodes, in an essay lamenting the passing of the keel, recalled the lack of literacy among the boating community.

"When I left school in 1907 at the age of 12, I was very fortunate for I could read and write; most of the keel lads could not. A good many families were reared on board and some of my friends had only a week or two schooling at a time; others none at all."

He noted some of the agents dealt with by keelmen were not kings of the pen themselves.

Memories of the camaraderie on the river were noted by Arthur Caldicott in a book, Life on the Trent and Humber Rivers (Richard Kay, Boston), re-

The maltings and chemical works at Barton, which stood on the site of today's Waters' Edge Country Park. Photo: Scunthorpe Telegraph. Middle: Vessels at the chemical works' jetty, Below: The Haven as it is today with the futuristic country park visitor's centre on the right.

viewed by the current author at the time. Mr Caldicott's family had the sloop Fanny.

"The river was a very friendly place, where you could always find friends at every mooring spot, waving and shouting greetings from along the banks as we passed.

"People knew everything that happened on the river and were quick to pass on news, whether good or bad."

Mr Caldicott recalled that his father Billie and uncle Ernest owned Fanny, which ran from Hull and was used on deliveries to villages along the Trent. From the age of nine he was expected to help with the work.

He said in the 1920s there were hundreds of barges, sloops and keels on the Trent and the United Towing Company had 10 or 12 tugs working on the river.

The winds could whip up the waters of the Humber and at Hull in such conditions a globe was raised to give mariners an indication of the wind.

Mr Caldicott recalled he and Tom Abbey, who by this time had bought the Fanny from the family, set sail from Hull, tacking to New Holland, but made only painful progress and eventually chose to drop anchor near Hessle. Everywhere below was submerged under two feet of water and they had to pump it out by hand.

"We were at it for hours and hours but when day broke we saw something that made us realise just how lucky we had been. About 500 yards from our position we could see what looked like the funnel and mast of a ship."

The ship was the Edgar Wallace, a trawler which had been on a 21-day trip to Bear Island and had been heading for St Andrew's Dock on January 9, 1935. She had dragged her anchor, hit a sand bank and turned over. Only three crew members survived. Mr Caldicott said it was probably the most frightening moment he experienced on the rivers. Fifteen men lost their lives and ironically a 16th following the capsizing of a tug called in to lift the vessel.

Two survivors, William Cameron and Clarry Wilcockson, were picked up by separate steamers and landed at Goole with the third, Charles Hendrick being picked up by a motor vessel and landed at Keadby.

Another tragedy in the Humber was on March 8, 1939, when the Lady Jeanette hit a sandbank while heading for St Andrew's Dock. The Lady Jeanette, which had been fishing off Iceland, was carried upstream by the tide and sank within seconds having hit a sandbank. Nine men were lost. She was owned by Jutland Amalgamated Trawlers Ltd of Hull and had around 1,400 kitts of fish on board at the time. The rescue operation included one of the Humber ferries, the Wingfield Castle.

A picture of life on the waterways is painted by Herbert Rhodes in a booklet Keel-a-hoy, produced by the Thorne Local History Society in 1993.

Herbert Rhodes recalled the sound of someone shouting 'keel-a-hoy' disappeared about 1940.

"It had been a familiar sound for longer than any living soul could remember. All around the docks of the River Humber seaports, the havens creeks and riverside quays, the warehouses, wharves and jetties - oh yes, far

The Barrow Market Sloop Toft Newton in Barrow Haven with Edgar Dawson's sloop alongside. The vessel is either loading or unloading with a derricking pole and gin wheel. The truck would be overladen if the sacks are 18 stone bags. Courtesy: HKSPS.

inland, wherever there was a navigable channel or canal one could find a wooden carvel-built, square rigged keel."

The carvel-built keels had flush planks of wood on the hull as opposed to clinker-built vessels, which had overlapping wood planks.

The arrival of steel-hulled barges with diesel engines in the 1920s led to the gradual disappearance of the old wooden vessels and even the steel hulled sail craft spurred on by government grants mostly converted to diesel power by the Second World War.

Mr Rhodes recorded: "The keels I skippered were built of wood, with iron keelsons, timbers, hooks, beams and outside hulls were of oak, the flat bottoms mainly of elm and decks of pine.

"The craft carried one mast and two square sails from which she took her name, also a pair of leeboards."

The masts could be dropped to pass under low bridges. He said the length of craft he sailed was usually about 61ft 6ins by 15ft 2ins or 4ins in width. Their deadweight capacity was between 120 and 130 tons.

"In the early 1900s the Sheffield and South Yorkshire Canal was alive with these small craft, loaded with all kinds of merchandise and minerals, hailing from Thorne, Stainforth, Hull, Goole, Beverley – in fact lots of small villages on the banks of the Ouse, Hull and Trent and navigations connecting them."

Mr Rhodes goes into great detail on the rigging holding the heavy cotton or flax canvas sails in place.

He said young men who became mates on the two man vessels had a lot to take in for it wasn't just a case of sailing a vessel but ensuring everything down below was shipshape.

"The skipper took him into the small cabin and showed him around, informing him that he had to learn to cook a good meal as well as keep his vessel clean and tidy. In the small cabin he found there were lockers, cupboards, drawers as well as a bunk – each containing different articles such as cooking utensils (frying pan and beefkettles), sewing twine, sail needles and palm, fog bell and horn, ship's papers and correspondence, small marlin spikes, coal and food, bedding and clothes, all below a swinging lamp. Each was stowed in its different place so that you did not get your food mixed up with the coal. There was also a small coal burning stove."

Mr Rhodes points out the above related to the skipper's cabin, which was at the after end of the ship. The mate's quarters were in the forecastle.

"It contained an oven and stove, a bunk and in different compartments was stowed the ship's gear, such as the topsail and sheets, the middle brace spare hatch covers, four navigation lamps, riding ball, two sets of pump gear, hand spike, marlin spike, fid, tar, calico, oakum, mallet and caulking irons, pitch kettle, mop and ladle , davit and blocks, second anchor , forelock and cotter pin, chain flitter (a chain stopper or sprag), a pair of rowlocks, dog leg (single-fluked kedge anchor for securing vessel to a

Owston Ferry Regatta in the 1920s or 1930s. Note the sloop on the right from which activities appear to have been conducted. The second photo shows yachts on the river at Owston.

canal bank), cathead, small kedge, handlings (handles for winches), paint, oil and two anchor chains – each about 30 fathoms in length."

The keel also carried two large anchors and a pair of wooden leeboards which were used for the same purpose as a centre board in a yacht, to stop the leeway when she was unloaded and under sail.

The earnings from the carriage of goods was known as freight and when he agreed to skipper a keel the arrangements were as follows.

"The owner to pay for the maintenance of the keel and gear insurance and such."

The owner's reward was a third of the keel's earnings while the skipper's duty was to find the cargoes and freights and pay the mate's wages, haulage costs, loading and discharging costs and victual the keel.

"The skipper's reward was the remaining two thirds of the freights."

He recalled the loading of coal from South Yorkshire collieries like Kilnhurst, Denaby and Manvers Main.

"They would proceed with the cargo to Hull, paying navigation dues and all expenses on their voyage. They would then sell the coal for the best price they could make to trawler owners, shipping firms or various mills.

"When the cargo had been discharged they paid the agreed amount to the skipper who would then pay the colliery agent for the coal. The money left over was the keel's freight."

Mr Rhodes recalled leaving his keel Britannia at Beverley and returning home to Thorne where his services were called upon by farmer John Mitchell.

"Old John said that he had 10 tons of nitrates of soda in Victoria Dock at Hull, and about 50 tons of tillage at Keadby tillage works. I then had to call at Garthorpe Shore and finish loading up with his spring corn, ploughs and harrows and other farm implements. When I was loaded up he wanted it taking to Rusham farm near Drax. I had to deliver the farm gear and three parts of the tillage there, the remaining tillage he wanted taking to New Bridge up the Aire and Calder."

Such cross transfer of goods was typical of both keel and sloop traffic and the sphere of trade for keels around the Humber is suitably outlined by Mr Rhodes as featured in the introduction.

"Main trade for keels was merchandise and raw materials from Hull to the industrial towns and cities. The return cargoes included coal, pitch, slag, steel and other finished products."

Mr Rhodes continued: "Sometimes we loaded a cargo of Trent sand and gravel dredged from the bed of the river by hand; the skipper would pay all expenses and when loaded the cargo belonged to him. He would then sell it to the best market, his customers being corporations, builders merchants, and contractors."

Great emphasis was placed on the knowledge gleaned by skippers and their crews over the years. Keelman Herbert Rhodes said it was impossible to learn the trade at nautical college; it could only be learned through the hard school of experience.

"The keel carried no maps or charts. He had to know the safe roadsteads in the rivers to ride at anchor, such as Hull Roads, Walter Dykes, Blacktoft Roads, Burr Wheel and Cliff End among others."

Different rivers had different depths at different times depending on the tide and the season. Passage was also dictated by the weight of cargo and the drafts in various canals. In 2010 passage of historic vessels up the Ouse and canals through to Leeds was limited because of the lack of rainfall, which meant water was at a premium.

We have already mentioned how the river traffic produced shipbuilding and other port activities. One of those industries was ropemaking, which left its mark in Barton-upon-Humber.

The prime ropemaker in Barton was Hall's Barton Ropery on the banks next to Barton Haven and close to today's Waters' Edge country park, which has been built on the site of the former maltings and chemical works which stood at the mouth of the haven as it opens into the Humber, a touch downstream from the bridge.

The Hall's were a north bank family rooted in the shipping trade. By the turn of the 19th century they had a fleet of 30 ships sailing from Hull, Whitby and London with family members moving into shipbuilding, sail making and vessel insurance.

The family was engaged in ropemaking in the Barton area from around 1767, with John, born in 1775, making the greatest contribution, despite his colourful career as a master mariner, merchant ship owner, privateer, whaler and gun runner to the Confederate states during the American Civil War.

The wars provided a market for ropes, sail cloth, twine and tarpaulin as did the growing fishing fleet sailing out of Hull in the middle of the 19th century, though demands from the whaling fleet were waning.

Locally grown materials were replaced by imported hemp and flax, with tar used to stop rope from rotting.

The firm was present at the Great Exhibition of 1851, boasting it was the manufacturer of patent-made cordage from Baltic hemp and patent made from Manilla Hemp, tarred.

John died in 1863, but the firm went on to quadruple its production before hard times bit. Nonetheless with the benefit of local demand, through shipping and fishing companies, the firm survived into the 20th century.

In the late 19th century it produced the largest coir rope made by machinery, 41 inches in circumference made up of 2,782 separate yarns. Coir was the fibre from the outer husk of the coconut.

The First World War produced a further demand for rope, as did the Second World War. The firm supplied the 16 inch tow ropes used to tow HMS Renown to the breakers yard and ropes that towed the Queen Elizabeth to be refitted for peace-time use. It is also believed Hall's rope was used by Sir Edmund Hilary in the conquest of Everest in 1953.

Despite moving with the times into the production of rope from synthetic fibres like nylon and polyester, ropemaking in the town came to an end in 1989.

Hall's Barton Ropery, which is believed to have supplied rope for the 1953 Everest expedition.

Other key industries around Barton Haven included whiting works, the malting works of Gilstrap Earps and the chemical works built to manufacture fertiliser in the 1870s which over the years had a number of names, including the Farmer's Company, ACC, Albright and Wilson and BritAg

The Humber Sloop and Humber Keel Regattas were days when rivermen showed off the pride in their vessels but sadly by the 1930s they had come to an end, though riverside sports and smaller scale regattas continued in small waterside communities for several decades after that.

Herbert Rhodes recalled: "Hull Keel Regattas were held in the 1890s when the keels were lined up riding at anchor opposite Hull Pier on the River Humber. A starting signal was given and the crews would then weigh anchor and set their sails to race round Burcome buoy near Grimsby. The finishing line was off the pier."

Mr Rhodes said that for such races the keels were manned by the skipper and four other men. Skippers had to show their skill in navigating their craft and harnessing the wind and tide.

He said the keel regattas ended in the early 1900s, though keelmen's aquatic sports continued on the canal at Thorne with the exception of the war years.

"Sports included swimming, greasy pole walking, sculling races, propelling a boat by hand with a crew of two or four men in the boat."

John Eyre of Scunthorpe, featured in a Riverside Nostalgia, noted crowds of 5,000 attended the festivities at Owston Ferry.

"Events were controlled by a loudspeaker and included swimming races, retrieving a flag from a greasy pole, a blindfold sculling race and a duck hunt featuring real ducks.

Mr Eyre said a number of the blindfold scullers did not know where they were going and would end up going down the river rather than across it. A mini revival of the regatta at Owston was held on July 19, 1986 and its programme recalled: "On 24th and 25th August 1874, the village of Owston Ferry held its annual Regatta. The secretary, Charles Gale, gave notice that a sailing boat race would take place - starting opposite John Leggott's Crooked Billet Inn, West Ferry. First class boats to round a boat moored opposite Burringham Ferry and back."

The programme recorded that the regatta sports of 1897 were hit by strong winds and the chief event of the 1900 regatta was a sailing race of about eight miles. Apart from the revival the last regatta was in 1939.

While the keels were scarce after the First World War the sloop racing in Barton continued through to 1929. Michael E Ulyatt in his book, Flying Sail, noted the start was off Barton Flats and continued around the middle

light vessel off Grimsby if the tide was on the ebb in the morning, if not they raced around the upper Whitton. As with the keels there were five people on board for the race.

He said the duration of the race depended on the wind and tide but took three to five hours. The winner received a medallion and a side of bacon and was allowed to carry a brass cockerel aloft for a year.

●If you have any waterways memories mail them to Chris Horan, 22 Priory Crescent, Scunthorpe, DN17 1HX. with name, address and contact details.

A medal from the riverside sports which from the image in the centre suggests it was from a keel regatta.

Chapter 7: Bridges and Ferries

TWO elements feature in this photo, courtesy of Brian Peeps of Barton. The image shows a silting up old creek from which the initial ferries across to Hull were run, while the second features the jetty and steam powered paddle boats from the across the water link which existed before the construction of the Humber Bridge. The jetty installations were completed in 1851.

WITHOUT doubt the greatest engineering achievement on the Humber was the building of the Humber Bridge, which at the same time was the death knell of the ferry link between New Holland and Hull.

The iconic paddle steamers won the affection of local people despite churning out air polluting grime and boasting a reliability record which at the best could be described as quaint.

The bridge took a decade in the building after a century of different types of crossing were mooted.

Meanwhile the most favoured ferries went to be museum pieces and bars/restaurants with the Lincoln Castle, once staged on the foreshore at Hessle, finally biting the dust in 2010, though at the time of publication there were calls for a new build/restoration.

Heading upstream the bridges at Keadby/Burringham on the River Trent and the railway bridge on the Ouse at Goole have had an eventful history, while downstream forts at the entrance to the River Humber show its strategic significance.

The Humber has long been a dividing line between Yorkies to the north

The light coloured vessel De Aston, registered in Grimsby, is seen alongside the former Clapson's shipyard with a sloop and to the right a steam barge, by the maltings in Barton Haven. Photo: Brian Peeps collection.

and Yellowbellies to the south, though across the centuries small ferries have provided a link, with the names of North and South Ferriby evident in the 12th century and ferry rights between the city of Kingston-upon-Hull and Barton, being conferred by King Edward II in 1316.

While Barton today seems an insignificant tributary into the Humber, for centuries it was a large port with its maritime pedigree evident from the calling up of ships and men in service of the king for both defence and mil-

A vessel being built for the Ministry of Defence at Clapson's Shipyard in Barton upon Humber. The port has provided ships for conflicts over the centuries. Photo: Brian Peeps.

A Humber bridge proposal put forward in 1948.

itary excursions abroad. The Social History and Antiquities of Barton, first published in 1856 by Henry Wm. Ball of Barton mentions a list of port towns contributing to the king's forces in 1359 for the invasion of Brittany. Significantly Barton has two entries, one as Barton-upon-Humber and the second as Barton-on-Humber. The demands on the latter were five ships and 91 men and the former three ships and 30 men.

The list also provides interesting information in relation to other ports on and around the Humber, with Hull providing 16 ships and 466 men, York providing one ship and nine men, Ravenspur one ship and 27 men, Stockwith (on the Trent) one ship and 10 men, Saltfleet two ships and 49 men, Grimsby 11 ships and 171 men, Boston 17 ships and 361 men.

Rights of ferry across the river were devolved through the king's bureaucracy by a system of governance and societal mores far removed from the layman's perception of public administration in the 21st century. Later references relating to Barton river crossings note that the abbots at Bardney monastery, on the River Witham near Lincoln, had rights of free passage across the Humber at Barton. Today there are arguments about the tolls on the Humber Bridge. In the past it was over what ferries were charging.

The above mentioned social history notes: "The Barton Ferry, as appurtenant to the manor, is valued in Domesday at 40s. The parties who managed the ferry even at this early period were accused of taking more toll than they were entitled to, the extractions being beyond the customary dues

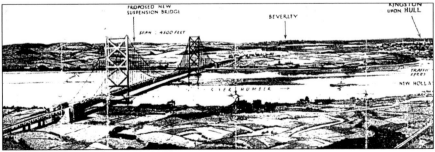

A bridge proposal put forward in 1948.

The Humber ferries ran a regular service between New Holland and Hull but were also renowned for their summertime cruises along the river. Day trippers on a ferry up the River Trent are captured here close to Owston Ferry. The vessel appears to be the Lincoln Castle.

which had been paid in the time of Edward the Confessor, a period which then appeared to be the standard of correct arrangement."

The terms of Edward I's ferry charter were general and did not name the port on the Lincolnshire side of the river but did set down charges.

"The passage fees were however fixed for every foot passenger at an obolus (one farthing) for every horse one penny and every cart with two horses 2d, and with three horses 3d and with four horses 4d."

A later treasury minute indicating the links across the Humber note the manner in which the ferry had to be provided: "One great boat with three men and cogboat belonging, and also one small boat with two men every market day, to serve either Hessle or to Hull as occasion shall require, every person paying one penny, every quarter of hard corn 2d, every quarter of malt 1d, one horse and man 6d, deals by the score 4d, nothing to be paid under a horse load; The boat or boats to return the next tide if weather serve, and not to take in stranger from Hull on the market day to the prejudice of the said inhabitants.

The conditions read: "Two or more of the boatmen to live at Barton. No boat to land on the green shore but in case of necessity. Also, upon request, neither boat to be denied to Hessle, paying the ancient fare, for every boat 5d and gift money 1d. No boat to lie at the horse staith landing, and also to land all passengers without paying any more than the customary due."

Around 1314 complaints were being made that too much was being taken by the ferry operators, resulting in the following answer from the authorities: "It is ordered by writ of our lord the king that they shall not on the passage on both sides the Humber permit toll to be taken for horse or foot passing the waters of the Humber more than has been accustomed to be taken."

The reply to another petition noted: "It is commanded by writ of the Lord the King that on the passage aforesaid on both sides of the Humber they shall take or permit to be taken for horse or foot on passing the water of Humber, for a horseman one penny, for a footman one halfpenny."

A full book could be written about the various ferries linking local communities across the Humber but in simple terms the last surviving ferry was that with a rail link from New Holland to Hull, though

Preliminary drilling work associated with the Humber Bridge was under way in 1967, as captured by Barton photographer David Lee of David Lee Photography Ltd, Falkland Way, Barton, tel (01652) 632451, mob 07968 168161. Email enquiries@davidleephotography.co.uk

market boats continued to run from Barton and other riverside communities to the commercial hub of Hull, into the 20th century.

Provision of a permanent crossing of the river had been mooted for more than century before it became a definite proposition in April 1969 when an announcement by the House of Commons Economic Affairs Secretary Peter Shore accepted that without a bridge, both banks of the Humber would lack the potential to expand. However, in local folklore it was a pledge at a Hull by-election in 1969 by leading Labour light Barbara Castle which really got things moving.

What she said was taken as a pledge to 'bribe' local voters. What she actually said was that the people would have their bridge as soon as a regional strategy in favour of it had been completed.

Economics Minister Peter Shore gave economic reasons for the bridge when he announced the go ahead for the project, saying: "I am sure that re-

The ferry landing at New Holland. Photo courtesy Brian Peeps.

gardless of what happens in the next few years the linking of both banks of the estuary will have profound repercussions on the area and any planning decisions taken."

The formal decision, once loose ends were tidied up, was taken by the Ted Heath Tory administration in 1971, when Environment Secretary Peter Walker said the government would lend 75 per cent of the cost of the bridge so that work could start at once. Local authorities either side of the bridge were partly responsible for shortfall. The estimated cost at the time with side roads was £23-million.

An alternative method of 'crossing' was noted by George Dow in his history of the Great Central Railway. He noted that in May 1882 there had been a proposal to tunnel under the Humber. The idea was promoted by Rowland and Charles Winn, who had iron ore interests on the south bank around Scunthorpe.

The proposed tunnel would have been used for a railway, passing through the Frodingham iron fields in the direction of Gainsborough.

At the same time there was a rival proposal for a bridge over the Humber promoted by the Hull and Lincoln Railway, crossing the Humber at Barton and with trains running to Lincoln.

The latter scheme was rejected but the railways were encouraged to work together to examine the realistic feasibility of a tunnel. As a result there were test borings at South Ferriby.

"Within a fortnight a depth of 102ft being reached through soil suitable for tunnelling and the North Eastern had begun similar operations at North Ferriby."

The ML and L railway secured powers to drill in the Humber in 1883 under the guidance of geologist Professor Boyd Dawkins.

The cost of driftways was estimated at £43,330 in 1885 but the development of alternative railway routes to Hull poured cold water on the scheme.

A railway bridge for the Humber had been proposed in 1883 by the Hull and Lincoln Railway Company. Had it gone ahead it would have been 5,900ft long with two central spans of 250ft each and 32 side spans of 150ft.

The proposals would have included a train deck 90ft above the river, the height of clearance being significant in that a lower bridge would have limited the passage of masted vessels, short of there being a swing or lift section. In days gone by the river traffic had priority and it took an Act of Parliament to override it, as happened with the Keadby lift bridge on the Trent in 1956.

Revived interest in a bridge was supported by the Grimsby Chamber of Commerce and Shipping in the 1920s and continued into the 1930s with the local authorities of the area contributing to the groundwork, Hull 25 per cent, Lindsey County Council (northern Lincolnshire) six and a quarter per cent, the East Riding £600, with smaller amounts from Grimsby, Bridlington, Hessle and Scarborough.

In 1931 a proposal for a multi-pier bridge was opposed by sloop and keel owner William Henry Barraclough, who said it posed a danger to shipping.

His submission casts light on the river trade at the time and how the mas-

The roadway taking shape on the Humber Bridge in 1980, courtesy of Frank Wressell, Wootton.

The final section being lifted into position on the Humber Bridge on June 19 1980 courtesy of Frank Wressell, Wootton, North Lincs.

ters of vessels had to contend with the turbulent waters, the wind and the moving sandbanks of the Humber, without the benefit of engines. His submission also highlights how movements of vessels were timed to co-incide with tides which would carry both sailing and lightly powered vessels up and down the river by the forces of nature.

The bridge proposal was of particular interest to Mr Barraclough, because he ran seven vessels as well as his own and was a director of the Hull Keel Lighter Owners' Mutual Insurance Association, which provided insurance for river craft on a mutual basis, meaning it met the cost of losses caused by accidents.

In a submission against the Bill for a bridge he said he had had 53 years of experience of sloops and keels on the river.

"My sloops are of the usual Humber Class, about 63ft long. Their masts are about 53ft, the height of the depth from the mast to the low water line is about eight feet. These sloops are fitted with a long gaff and when sailing the top of the gaff is above the top of the mast.

"The gaffs are about 31ft and the height of the gaff when the sail is set would be some 12ft to 15ft above the mast head so that my vessels when light are from the water line to the top of the gaff, 75ft in height. The vessels cannot sail properly under control unless the gaff is set.

"The keels will vary from 55ft to 60ft from the water line, but they have a square rigged sail so that the sail, being a square sail, does not go above the mast when they are sailing.

"My sloops carry between 125 and 140 tons as they vary slightly in size and my keels, which are about 57ft long, carry about 80 tons.

"I have considered the proposal for the bridge and in my opinion it will be a dangerous obstacle to all navigation and will be fatal to the sailing vessels on the river.

"I do not propose to deal with the effect of the bridge upon steamer navigation, but it is at any rate obvious that in hazy weather the bridge will be an absolute danger to steamers."

A particular aspect of the bridge design, which envisaged a number of pillars in the water, was that its emphasis was on creating a crossing without sufficient regard to the manoeuvrability of vessels on the river, sailing craft having to track across the channel.

Back in the 1930s it was common to see lighters and sail vessels being pulled up river to the Ouse and Trent against the tide, attached to trailing lines, by a team of tugs.

Mr Barraclough noted: "With regard to the tugs and tows, the tugs on the Humber tow as many as eight river craft at a time in two strings – four on each – and they will then stretch from the stem of the tug to the stern of the last tow, between 700ft and 800ft.

"As the navigation of these tugs on the river is tidal and they have to proceed with the tide, it is not possible always to keep the last tow in line with the tug, beside being on two strings the rows are spread out behind the tug,

Passengers make their way along the landing ferry at New Holland.

so there is over 100ft distance between the port and the starboard side of the last two tows.

"Owing to the strong tidal running in the Humber and the heavy seas, when the wind is against the tide, the last vessels cannot be kept always straight behind the tugs.

"In my opinion there would be grave danger of some of these tows from time to time coming into contact with the piers of the bridge."

Mr Barraclough recalled an incident in which a vessel under tow had come into collision with what was described as the Hessle Light Float.

He said his main trade was between Hull and Barton and Brigg so his vessels and others like them were rarely towed.

"In particular I have a large trade with Barton Haven and with Ferriby Sluice. In my opinion the bridge will kill the trade between Hull and Barton Haven.

"Owing to the fact that the headway given by the bridge on the south side of the river varies from 65ft to 35ft, there will be no room at any of these arches for my sloops to get through when sailing. This will mean that the sailing vessels will have to make for the main 900ft span in order to get enough headroom.

"If such a vessel is coming up the river from Hull to Barton and there is a favourable wind she will no doubt be able to get through the 900ft span, but having got through the 900ft span I do not think it would be possible for her to get to Barton Haven on the same tide."

Missing the tide meant the vessel would lose 12 hours in her schedule. Vessels leaving Barton Haven could similarly be held up.

He highlighted the limitations of Barton as a port: "Vessels can only reach or leave the jetties at Barton or Barton Haven at high water or within about half an hour of high water.

"When such a vessel gets out of the haven, if the bridge is there, she will have difficulty in getting to the navigable span unless there is an easterly wind to take her to the

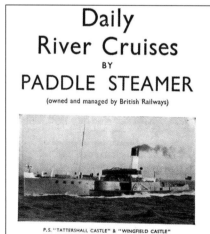

**Daily
River Cruises**
BY
PADDLE STEAMER
(owned and managed by British Railways)

P.S. "TATTERSHALL CASTLE" & "WINGFIELD CASTLE"
FROM
ROYAL DOCK BASIN, GRIMSBY
THROUGHOUT THE SEASON
(Weather and other circumstances permitting)

A day cruising on the ferry was something to look forward to for many local people.

Yorkshire side and then she will have a head wind to make the bridge opening. "I think the result will be that these vessels will also miss a tide before they can get an 'offing' and make safely for the bridge.

"If it is suggested that these vessels can go through the southern spans of the bridge with their masts down, I say this is impossible if the vessels are loaded as to lower the masts would mean that

Corporation Bridge lifts for the Lincoln Castle to pass into Alexandra Dock, Grimsby, her final resting place.

the hatch covers would have to be off, and in the seas that run at that part this would be unsafe for the ship and cargo when loaded."

The bridge had been proposed to cross the river at what was known as Hessle Whelps and Barton Bulldogs, which Mr Barraclough pointed out was the roughest part of the river.

"This is due no doubt to the strong current that sets through there, making up to seven knots an hour and the seas that are set up whenever the wind is against the tide. These seas make the command of a sailing ship difficult when staying at the end of a tack and results in missing stays.

"At present vessels keep out of the worst water by keeping either to the Yorkshire or Lincolnshire shore in accordance with the state of the wind."

He said if the bridge was built all traffic would have to pass through the central span.

"When a sloop is beating up with the tide against the wind, she will be put in danger, first because the sea way when coming about for the bridge she may come into the wind and become unmanageable for the time being and be carried on to the abutments. Further she will have to come about at inconvenient times for the purpose of making the bridgeway, and she may be in danger of collision with steamers or other vessels coming up at the same time.

"At present sloops are accustomed to sail straight through from Barton Haven to Hull, or from Hull to Barton Haven. Now they will always have to go through the bridge on the Yorkshire side.

"My opinion is the construction of this bridge will cause an increase of sand on the Barton side and cause the Barton Haven and the jetties at Barton to be silted up."

He went on: At present my experience is that the first of the ebb runs from the windmill at Hessle across to New Holland. I remember when there was a deeper channel than there is at present on the south side of the river opposite Hull. This channel came out at about Hedon Haven, and the ebb ran very strong through it.

"From my knowledge of the Humber I am quite certain that the 15 piers placed in the Humber will have some effect upon the sands in the neighbourhood, though I do not know what the exact effect will be.

"There will be eddies at all the piers. I know there is an eddy just above Chalder Ness (Chowder Ness) on the flood tide which stretches from the beacon at Chalder Ness to about Ferriby Hall."

Mr Barraclough, who lived at Barton for 48 years, said the proposed location of the bridge was in an area which suffered from fog, with steamers bound for Goole anchoring up because when the fog cleared it was too late to catch the tide.

"It is a bad place for fog. Sometimes when we have left Hull in clear weathers we have run into fog which comes from the south channels and then if you are able to find your way you sometimes get it clear again about Whitton Ness.

" I have sailed the Humber from Spurn right up the whole length and in my opinion the site of the proposed bridge is the worst which could have been chosen, from a navigation point in the whole stretch of the river."

Mr Barraclough also raised the possibility of a vessel hitting one of the piers and sinking, not only damaging the bridge but sinking and blocking the channel.

"In bad weather, our class of vessel when she gets in the heavy sea at Hessle, becomes difficult to manage until they get drifted up or down the

A string of keels is towed up the River Trent past Burton Stather.

river where it is smoother water, when we again get control."

A Bill was presented to Parliament by Hull and Lindsey in the early 1930s to seek powers for a bridge authority to enable plans for a crossing to be progressed.

The building of the Golden Gate Bridge in San Francisco in 1935 led to suggestions for a similar suspension bridge across the Humber and there were various proposals followed, one with an illustration in 1948.

Local authorities in the area

PS Frodingham formerly Dandy Dinmont.

continued to promote the logic of a bridge and in 1959 a Humber Bridge Act was passed by Parliament. It established a Humber Bridge Board with real powers to prepare for a bridge.

Securing permission for a bridge was one thing, actually building it was another, as was found out during a difficult construction which delayed the opening to 1981, when commemorative mugs and other items had been made for a couple of years earlier. One such mug is displayed by the cottage museum in Hornsea, having been made by the former Hornsea Pottery.

At the official opening of the Humber Bridge the Queen remarked: "It is quite clear from the very first sight of this bridge that it is not only its size, but also its beauty, which makes it such a splendid advertisement for British engineering."

The bridge on its opening was the longest single span suspension bridge in the world, with a main span of 1,410 metres, a 30 metre clearance over high water, a deck width of 28.5 metres (including footpaths) and a tower height of 155.5 metres.

The construction had involved the use of 480,000 tonnes of concrete and 27,500 tonnes of steel in the road deck and cables.

Despite the comments of the Queen it had not been a totally smooth operation, with the biggest problem encountered in establishing a stable footing for the south bank tower, which is actually in the river itself.

July, 1972, saw the first earthworks under way preparing the link roads

A car boards the diesel powered Farringford, the last vessel to run on the New Holland to Hull route. Right: Vessels on a ferry crossing the river.

for the bridge and in March 1973 work began on anchorage and tower foundations. The north tower was completed in 1974 and by 1975 work had started in Priory Park, Hull, on construction of the road sections, which would be sailed upstream to be lifted into position on suspension cables.

Two water tight chambers called caissons were constructed on the south bank in 1975 but failed to cut their way into the river bed as simply as engineers had hoped and 3,000 tonnes of steel ingots were brought in from British Steel in Scunthorpe to lay across the caissons to force them to sink into the bed of Kimmeridge clay.

The sinking process had also been affected by underground water, which was washing away liquid bentonite used to ease the downward passage of the caissons. In addition to the steel ingots, around 2,000 tonnes of extra concrete was also fed into each caisson and remains in the structure, the steel having been removed after the caissons had eventually sunk and stabilised.

In November 1975 a brass and copper time capsule with copies of local papers, a £1 note and 50p piece was laid in the foundations of the south bank tower in a special bottoming out ceremony. The cylinder was placed in the tower by the Bridge Board's chairman, Councillor Alex Clarke.

The south bank tower was completed in 1976 and was handed over to British Bridge Builders for the next stage of construction, which included the linking of the two banks with catwalks between the towers. Cable spinning between the two banks began in September 1977. The cable spinning was completed in June 1979 and in October the first of 124 box sections was moved from Hull ready to be hoisted into position on suspension cables in mid river. Welding together the box sections began in February 1980 and there was almost a disaster in March that year when one of the lifting gantries on the bridge broke away, causing damage and leaving two road sections dangling in mid air. The final section of the roadway was hoisted into place and hung from cables in July. Welding of the deck sections was completed in December with work on the asphalt surface of the road section having started in September.

The bridge was opened to traffic on June 24, 1981, but not without incident, the opening being delayed by a bomb scare. The lead article in the Scunthorpe Telegraph carried the headline in capital letters: "BOMB SCARE ON THE BIG DAY."

Journalists Pat Otter and Keith Scrivener in their report relayed the shock news: "The Humber Bridge is open. But the inaugural ceremony was dramatically delayed by 30 minutes today after a telephone call to the Press Association in London that a bomb had been planted on the complex.

"Police evacuated the control block and cleared traffic while they carried out a thorough search. Then at noon the all clear was given and the opening ceremony put into motion."

There had also been a hoax on the day of the official opening, which was well remembered by operations manager John Oxley who said: "There was a bomb scare. We found out who it was. It is a good job the police got the culprit first before my staff."

The opening was performed by the Humber Bridge Board chairman

Although linked by ferries for centuries and trade between the north and south banks, the opening of the bridge in 1981 heralded permanent links between the Yorkies and Yellowbellies, though even today there remains strong local rivalry and banners such as those sported above are not too far off the mark.

Coun Alex Clarke, who paid the first £1 toll at the Hessle end to attendant John Mackindas of Immingham and then drove across the bridge with the board's vice-chairman, Coun George Ferriby of Barton. Once the car had returned to Hessle the police simultaneously at both ends lifted barriers to allow queues of traffic to flow over the bridge.

The progress of the bridge building was followed by freelance photographer David Lee of Barton. His business, now based in Falkland Way, Barton, although much more diverse than bridge images, is almost synonymous with the structure with a Pandora's box of atmospheric shots having been produced, some of which appear on the firm's website.

The first palpable evidence of a serious attempt to build the bridge was witnessed in 1967, when his photos of test drilling on the Humber made front page news.

The Barton born and bred photographer was engaged by bridge consultants Freeman, Fox and Partners to keep a record of developments on the southern side of the bridge, which inevitably gave him access to the construction site on a regular basis, though there were some hair-raising moments, including one occasion when he was hoisted in a cement bucket on the end of a crane, to capture pictures of the caissons under construction off Barton. Health and safety regulations would almost certainly today have ruled out such a method of gaining a vantage point.

Another hairy occasion he recalled was being on the cross beam between two catwalks waiting for the first road section to be brought by barge from the construction yard at Priory Park. The delivery was delayed by the tides but he had to remain at his perch for several hours, despite the cold.

Even today he remains fascinated with the structure and takes pride in the fact he worked on the bridge in his own specialism, as did other people in the locality in theirs.

The crew of either the Wingfield or Tattershall Castle in the 1950s which made pleasure trips to Spurn Point for 12 weeks during the summer. Front from the left: Claud Dawson, Captain Dobbs, unknown, steward Ron Turner and two unnamed women assistants. Back: Chris Braithwaite (contributor), Stan Johnson, Colin Richardson, Les Claxton, Lol Clayton, unknown. Mr Braithwaite recalled there were one or two trips a year up the river towards Goole.

ThE Lincoln Castle, in 1975, with damage to her port side sustained on the ebb tide when she was at Hull pontoon before leaving for New Holland at 7.30am, her second trip. The first boat from Hull was 6.30am and the last boat from New Holland was 10.30pm.

David noted the building of the bridge had changed Barton, turning it into something of a tourist spot, further enhanced by the opening of the Waters' Edge country park which encompasses the former site of chemical works and maltings and is adjacent the former ropery.

As part of his education in the mid-1950s David attended the Gregg School in Hull and like many others on the south bank went to school on the paddle ferries from New Holland. He would take the 7.50am train to New Holland and the 8.10am ferry across the Humber, catching paddle steamers which in those days included the Tattershall Castle, the Wingfield Castle and the Lincoln Castle.

Today the Wingfield is based by the Historic Quay complex at Hartlepool, where she and the Tattershall Castle were built, the latter now being a bar on the Thames in Westminster, not far from the Houses of Parliament. Despite efforts to save her, the Lincoln Castle, based in Alexandra Dock, Grimsby, was dismantled in 2010.

The ferry crossings came to an end the same day the Humber Bridge opened to traffic, with the last journey being made by the less iconic diesel powered Farringford.

The Tattershall Castle ended her service in 1972 and it was the end of the line for the Wingfield Castle on March 4, 1974. The vessel was named after the home of the De La Pole family on the north bank.

The Wingfield Castle had been commissioned to be built by Sir William Gray and Co, Hartlepool. It was 210ft long with a beam of 57ft. On her retirement the Scunthorpe Telegraph noted the Hull skipper Stan Wright lamenting her passing: "I can

Photographer David Lee of Barton, who through his pictures chronicled the building and life of the Humber Bridge, from before its inception through to today.

only say it is with remorse that I am leaving her," he said.

The next day the paper reported: "It was never 100 per cent certain that the 5.31pm departure from Coronation Pier would be the last. Only with hours to go was the final decision taken when the Lincoln Castle returned to service after a refit."

Mr Lee recalled occasions when he and others were late for school because of the tides and ferries having to divert along a longer route because of sandbanks near the surface.

For those who used the ferries on a regular basis other delays to the service were caused by fog and ice on the river. The paddles on the steamers were also regularly damaged by items flowing downstream or upstream in the river. The ferries were designed so they could sit on the sandbanks if need be but for commuters this was obviously a great inconvenience for if they became stranded they would have to wait until the next tide to float off the sandbank.

Dorothy Taylor (nee Bennett), who was brought up in Barton, recalled moving on from Barton Grammar School to Wood's Commercial College in Springbank West, Hull. Her journey to the college was often hit by fog and on some days she and other pupils were stuck on the south bank until midday and then would phone the college principal, who would then give them permission to go home.

Mrs Taylor recalled the bad winter of 1946/47 when there were ice floes on the Humber.

"Ice was floating down the Humber in huge chunks and we were sitting downstairs. The noise these huge chunks of ice made against the side of the ferry was very frightening."

Colour picture parade

An atmospheric shot of the Humber Bridge taken by David Lee. This image and others by David Lee, courtesy David Lee Photography Ltd. Details enquiries@davidleephotography.co.uk David Lee Photography Ltd. Tel 01652 632451. Mob. 07968 168161.

Colour picture parade

The sloop Comrade and the Humber Bridge. Photo: Lesley Everatt.

The South-cliffe after taking delivery of her new sails.

Colour picture parade

Building the cofferdams: Photo: David Lee Photography Ltd.

Colour picture parade

The Humber bridge at sunset taken from South Ferriby.

Children celebrated the official opening of the bridge on July 17, 1981, by the Queen

Colour picture parade

Sections of roadway are lifted into place: Photo: David Lee Photography Ltd.

Colour picture parade

Above: David Lee's photo of the completed Humber Bridge looking towards Hessle.
Left: Phyllis sets off from Alexandra Dock, Hull, for the Parade of Sail.

The sign signals the end of the line for theformer Humber ferry, Lincoln Castle.

Colour picture parade

A sunset over the Humber near Goxhill Haven. Below: The sun sets on the Lincoln Castle, pictured as dismantling work started in Alexandra Dock, Grimsby in 2010.

Colour picture parade

The Tattershall Castle on the Thames in London

The Wingfield Castle which is now at the Historic Quay in Hartlepool (inset).

During the Second World War the Humber Ferries were used to evacuate children from Hull to rural communities on the south bank, which given the heavy bombing of Hull, appears to have been sound thinking. Vessels involved in the evacuation included the Wingfield Castle, the Tattershall Castle and the Killingholme.

Chris Braithwaite, who worked for the ferries, recalled: "They had bags and their little gas masks and name tags and there was a lot of excitement."

The last crossing of the Lincoln Castle was in 1978 and followed a dry dock inspection which revealed severe structural deterioration of her boilers. She had been sharing the route with the former Isle of Wight diesel ferry Farringford, which was left to soldier on alone pending the opening of the Humber Bridge, which as previously mentioned was expected to be opened earlier than it was.

The Lincoln Castle, built in 1940 at the yard of A and J Inglis on the Clyde in Scotland, was established as a restaurant on the foreshore of the Humber at Hessle, but this was short lived and after suggestions she be moved to Cleethorpes beach, she eventually found a home in Alexandra Dock, Grimsby. However, the iconic vessel was broken up during late summer 2010, having served as a bar/restaurant close to the National Fishing Heritage Centre.

A combination of dock charges and the deteriorating state of the vessel appear to have combined to motivate owner Colin Johnson, to send her on a voyage into history.

According to reports, insurers had indicated they would no longer be able to insure the paddle steamer and contractors H Cope and Sons were contracted to dismantle the vessel, which in addition to working the ferry route from New Holland to Hull had also, with other paddle steamers, been the venue for days out up and down the Humber.

In addition to taking in the fresh air they attracted passengers because the bar was open all day in an era when pubs had limited hours, obliging them not to open until lunchtime and to close for a period in the afternoons.

Mr Johnson is reported to have said the vessel was in danger of sinking in 2007 and various bodies, including local authorities, maritime trusts and preservation societies had been offered the ferry. However, surveys found extensive corrosion which would have cost £3-million to rectify. In order to repair the vessel it would have had to be taken from the dock to a dry dock elsewhere. He said the engines were in good condition and had been advertised for £20,000 but no owner had been found.

The keen observer would have also recalled the difficulties in moving the Lincoln Castle into Alexandra Dock in the first place following the construction of the A180 road bridge. The new bridge had reduced the height of vessels putting into the dock requiring special measures to be taken.

To overcome the problem the superstructure of the Lincoln Castle, including her bridge and funnel, were cut away in a major operation at Immingham's Graving Dock and in 1987 the hull of the vessel was towed under the bridge and through the raised Corporation Bridge into Alexandra Dock, followed by the restoration of the upper part of the vessel.

The vessel had been one of three planned jointly in the late 1930s by the North Eastern Railway Company and Hull Corporation at a cost of £125,000, £30,000 being paid by Hull.

Stephen Sharpe, chairman of the Lincoln Castle Preservation Society, said it had in vain offered the owner £104,000, which it considered was more than she was worth.

Following the dismantling he accepted there was little to be achieved through squabbling, saying: "In the end it will not bring the Lincoln Castle back, instead we move on and aim to build a New Lincoln Castle. This boat will be built on the Humber and will involve companies from both the north and south banks.

"Hull will be the prime site as this is where our dry dock will be. The dock has a Grade II preservation order on it and this is eligible for lottery grants - preservation and educational funding.

"Further we will be able to offer apprenticeship courses. We will also be able to offer work experience for prisoners nearing the end of their time. This coupled with the jobs available to local companies makes a very high profile image," he said.

"The New Lincoln Castle will be presented in the colours and style she carried in the 1950s when operated by the Associated Humber Lines."
He said the vessel would have a steel welded hull rather than being riveted.

"She will also be built to modern health and safety regulations. She will also be environmentally friendly as well as having easy access to the less able passengers, otherwise she will be built to the original plans which we have."

Tickets for the final crossing of the Farringford were snapped up like hot cakes. She was no longer the non steaming poor relation of the ferry but the final flag carrier of a century and a half of powered sailing across the river, on a route which dated back centuries.

While cars and foot passengers were the order of the day in 1981 over the centuries the ferry and others along the Humber carried both sheep and cattle across the river, with the Hessle to Barton route being one of the drivers routes from the north to the south.

Fog was always a problem on the Humber and in August 1958 there was a collision between the Lincoln Castle and the Wharton Shipping vessel

The Lincoln Castle in 2010, in the early stages of being dismantled.

Lizzonia off Hull Corporation pier. Gangway doors on the ferry were ripped open and rails torn away on the vessel's first crossing of the day.

Damage was superficial but it had been a shock for passengers, one of whom recalled hearing a blast on the vessel's siren: "I knew something was wrong and then saw the head of the Lizzonia coming towards the doors where the cars go off."

During fog in March 1951, the Lincoln Castle was put out of service, having been hit by the Tattershall Castle.

In respect of the collision one passenger stoically remarked: "It was just one of those alarming experiences that could have been very much worse. Luckily there were not many people aboard either vessel. Had there been, then I feel sure someone could have been badly injured."

Florence Parkin, in a Riverside Nostalgia publication, recalled visiting her grandmother at Barrow on Humber, travelling on the ferry from Victoria Pier, Hull.

"We thought it rather exciting as we came on the train along the water's edge on the north side of the Humber and it was our first glimpse of water for us. We had come from the cotton mill town of Bolton in Lancashire."

She said her grandfather always met them at Paragon Station in Hull and they took a tram to the ferry pier.

"We always rushed to kneel on the forms and look down into the engine room. How shiny all the brasswork was. You could tell the engineers had a pride in their job.

Sometimes there were cows on board as farmers from Lincolnshire used to go to Hull Cattle Market. The cows were always roped off to one end of the ferry.

"As soon as the ferry started up we rushed to the side of the boat to see the wash. I used to call it soap suds."

On another occasion the ferries were used by amateur film makers in Burton-upon-Stather as the setting for their films with footage shot on the ferries themselves.

The history of the New Holland route is recalled in Alan A D'Orley's book The Humber Ferries.

The ferry service from New Holland developed from very humble beginnings. The first service was begun by a man named Thomas Dent soon after 1803 from an isolated creek close to the later day rail ferry terminal.

The creek had been known for other trade, as reported in the Lincoln, Rutland and Stamford Mercury.

"The isolated position of the spot, the paucity of inhabitants, with other collateral advantages, pointed it out as an eligible place for the debarkation of smuggled goods, but more especially Holland's gin, and it was notoriously used as such; hence it obtained the name of New Holland.

"In 1825, the Hull Corporation which owned the ferry from Hull to Barton and was lessee of the Crown Ferry from Barton to Hull, learned the competing company proposed to establish a ferry from Barrow to Hull and run coaches from Barrow to London, competing against those from Barton waterside."

In due course Joseph Brown of Barton and other people combined to buy land at Oxmarsh Creek in Barrow and formed a company known as the New Holland Proprietors, with the aim of developing a new crossing from New Holland.

"Crossings on the official ferry (then the Royal Charter) had increased to four crossings from Barton each day."

The competing ferry was not as efficient and there were reports of a sailing vessel being used on the route. While traffic increased through Barton, so did the price of the ferry.

"James Ackland, a reform agitator, maintained the Hull Corporation and their tenants could not legally charge more than a half penny a passenger, which was the fixed amount in the Charter granted by King Edward more than five centuries before.

"In September 1831, Ackland started his opposition ferry in a vessel called the Public Opinion between Hull and Barton, at a half penny a crossing, taking trade from the official ferry which paid £800 a year for the

A Humber ferry ploughs its way through the ice-floes on the river.

crossing rights.

"The Corporation asked for an injunction to restrain Ackland but this was refused."

However, his upstart ferry came to an end on economic grounds as it had cost him £350 in fighting the battle.

The Barton route was hit by the fading away of coach services following the arrival of railways and the river crossing by the vessel Magna Charta from New Holland became more popular because of the shorter route.

"By 1832 the Magna Charta was providing a three times a day service to Hull and with the increased traffic it was decided to build a jetty to overcome the difficulty of mud flats."

In 1846 the number of travellers passing through New Holland was put at 70,000, a figure which increased with rail links to the ferry, which was eventually run by British Rail.

In addition to respectfully, sounding its horn, following the restoration to sail of Comrade, the Lincoln Castle and the other paddle steamers had a sometimes eventful history.

Mr Braithwaite, who lived in Barton, worked for the London and North Eastern railways on servicing the ferries between 1939 and 1981 and in his memories recalled the vessels needed to take in plenty of water to keep the boiler pressure up but in one bad winter the water supplies at both Hull and New Holland had frozen up.

"The ferries were kept running by firemen from Hull laying out pipes

The old rail bridge across the Trent at Burringham, opened to traffic in 1864.

from Queen Street at Hull, across the dock to provide the ferries with a water supply."

Mr Braithwaite related details of day to day work on the ferries done in the workshops: "Various things went wrong now and again with new bearings and new bushes being fitted. Sometimes the floats or paddles needed replacing because they hit things in the river or had worked loose. It was general wear and tear but they had to be maintained."

He particularly recalled fruiterers from the south bank attending the fruit market in Hull and having their goods wheeled to the ferry and along the jetty at New Holland, prior to distribution to the villages.

Mr Braithwaite recalled the vessels being involved in a couple of royal visits, though on one occasion the Queen and the Duke of Edinburgh simply walked across the Wingfield Castle to access the launch to take them to the Royal Yacht Britannia, which was in King George V Dock.

He said the ferries were able to carry cattle because they had pens for pigs, horses and cattle. In the early days cars were hoisted onto the ferries by crane but by 1934 both Hull and New Holland had floating pontoons which allowed cars to be driven on and off the ferries.

Mr Braithwaite said the Lincoln Castle could take around 20 cars with the Wingfield and Tattershall Castles accommodating 17 cars.

Up until December, 1957 cars being transported across by ferry were charged by horsepower rather than by length. It was announced the single fare for second class passengers was to go up from 1s to 1s 3d for a single journey and the saloon fare from 1s 6d to 1s 9d. Return fares were double the single fares.

Vehicle fares were set at 11s 6d for single journeys and £1 1s return for vehicles up to 13ft 6ins and 16s 6d single and £1 10s return for vehicles 15ft 6ins. Longer vehicles were charged £1 1s 6d single and £1 19s return. Three wheeled vehicles were reclassified with a charge of 10s single and 18s 6d return.

Mr G B Pears of the British Transport Commission in Hull said: "We decided to base our charges on length instead of horse power because many vehicle owners do not know the horse power of their vehicles. We now

The King George V rail bridge widely known as Keadby Bridge. Photo courtesy: Bryan Longbone.

have a more up to date method of charging fares for vehicles in the same way that Channel ports do."

The fares for vehicles had been 10s 2d single for those up to 10 horse power with a return fare of £1 0s 4d. Vehicles of 10 to 20 horse power were charged at 14s 8d single and £1 9s 4d return. Vehicles of more than 20 horse power were charged 19s single and £1 18s return.

While the Humber Bridge attained top ranking in terms of world construction, the building of other bridges along the key water routes had an effect on waterside communities and ferries across the rivers.

Up until 1864 the furthest downstream bridge on the Trent was the Gainsborough toll bridge, which was built in 1787 at a cost of £1,200, levying tolls through to 1932. An Act of Parliament for the Burringham rail bridge was passed in 1861 and the structure was designed by Charles Bartholomew to be 484ft long by 25ft with a 160ft swing section.

The bridge, was replaced in 1916 by the King George V road and rail bridge a stones throw downstream. A presentation on the bridge was made to the Institution of Civil Engineers by James Benjamin Hall. He reported: "Keadby Bridge on the Great Central Railway, carries the main line traffic from Liverpool, Manchester and Sheffield, and the heavy coal traffic from the South Yorkshire coalfields, to the ports of Immingham and Grimsby, across the River Trent, about 14 miles north of Gainsborough.

"It replaces an old swing railway bridge which has existed for upwards of 60 years and carries also a public highway connecting the townships of Keadby and Gunness.

●The principal feature of the bridge is the lifting span which is the heaviest yet constructed in Europe, having a total weight of approximately 3,000 tons.

●For some time before the work was undertaken, the condition of the

The old rail bridge was dismantled after the new Keadby bridge was opened. This image shows both bridges in August 1920. Photo: courtesy Bryan Longbone.

old structure had given rise to some considerable anxiety, and the projected opening of Immingham Dock in 1912, together with the development of the South Yorkshire coalfields and the resulting heavy and increasing traffic, rendered it imperative that the renewal of the bridge should be undertaken without further delay.

●Accordingly a scheme was prepared early in 1910 for building a new bridge about 58 chains north of the old one and diverting the railway at this point, and steps were taken to obtain the necessary powers under a Bill before Parliament. Owing to the opposition offered principally by the shipping interests, the Bill was subsequently withdrawn; but finally after further opposition from various interest, authority was obtained from the Board of Trade enabling the company to carry out the work on its present site, adjacent to the old bridge.

●The railway company undertook among other things to provide a public highway across the bridge and to give the main river channel on the east side a clear waterway of 150ft, which was equal to the two existing channels of 60ft together with the centre pier and dolphin upon which the old swing span turned.

●The report said that no doubt the Royal Commission on canals and inland waterways had some influence on the river authority's requirements for improvement of the Trent waterway to give direct access from the sea to Nottingham had been considered for some time.

●The scheme as carried out involved the construction of a deviation railway about two miles in length, connecting the existing lines on each side of the river and crossing it on a line parallel with the old bridge and about 200ft from it on the north or downstream site.

●To assess the most suitable bridge for the purpose, visits were made to Canada and the United States, with the Scherzer type of rolling lift bascule for the opening span being selected.

●The decision was influenced by the need to keep the river channel open during construction and the ability to construct the lifting span in the opening position.

The bridge at Keadby in its near erect state. Photo courtesy of Bryan Longbone.

"The bridge being situated at a bend in the river, navigation is rendered somewhat difficult by the set of the tides, the varying channel and the swiftness of the current which runs at five to seven knots at ebb and flow."

The report also noted the added difficulties caused by the tidal bore or aegir at the period of greatest spring tides.

"Observations taken on one of these occasions showed that the speed of the wave was nearly 15 miles an hour; this was quite a phenomenal tide, with everything, including the wind, favourable to a big bore.

●"During construction, with the old and new structures existing side by side, the problem of ensuring safe navigation through the bridges was a difficult one, and only through a very carefully arranged system of signals and guide piling between the old dolphins and the new bridge piers, supplemented by a steam tug in constant attendance day and night, which was provided at the insistence of the river authorities and the Board of Trade to assist vessels requiring its aid in navigating through the openings of the two

Workmen pose for a photo while dismantling the swivel section of the old rail bridge across the Trent in September, 1920. Photo Bryan Longbone collection.

bridges, was the work brought to a satisfactory conclusion, without accident to vessels."

The clear headway under the two fixed river spans is 18ft above high water and low water of ordinary spring tides is 14ft.

The overall length of the bridge between the faces of the east and west abutments is 548ft.

The four river piers and the east and west abutments are constructed of blue brick and granite. The piers have concrete hearting and are founded on steel caissons filled with concrete which in all cases was carried down to a depth of 50ft below low water, where a foundation was obtained in the red Keuper Marl. The abutments rest upon beds of concrete 6ft thick, reinforced with old rails, the foundations to which are closely piled.

The total weight of the steelwork in the bridge is 2,760 tons, and the quantity of steelwork sunk permanently in the foundation caissons is 590 tons.

The lifting span of the bridge was worked electrically by motors carried on the leaf (opening section) itself, the power being transmitted through spur gear to the operating pinions at each side of the moving leaf. These pinions engage with horizontal fixed racks, 40ft in length, mounted on braced supports carried on the piers, this length being equal to the travel of the pinion necessary to open the bridge to its fullest extent, namely through a vertical angle of 81 degrees 51 minutes, which angle is determined by the vertical projection of the river face of pier no3. The time taken to open or close the bridge by electrical power is less than two minutes.

The first of the supporting piers was built on the eastern side of the river but encountered problems when it began to slip into the river.

"The first serious difficulty encountered during the progress of the works was met in sinking this caisson, which was commenced in December 1912, and towards the end of January 1913, a movement of the mass towards the river was detected."

In addition to movement towards the river as the caisson sank into soft material, a tilt had begun to appear which brought the caisson about 2.5 inches out of plumb. "During the next two or three days the movement increased to such an extent that the whole mass moved 3ft 3ins out of position and 12.5 inches out of plumb, of which about 10 inches occurred during one night. The total weight of the caisson and its concrete filling at the time of this occurrence was approximately 2,000 tons. The actual land on the river bank appeared to be slipping.

"Additional piles were then driven on the riverside, a screen of close pile sheeting was driven at a rake some distance inshore, and the caisson was anchored back to these piles. The steps thus taken were effective in arresting any further movement, but in view of the treacherous nature of the ground, it was decided to revert to the original design by adding an additional 70ft span on the east side, so as to keep the weight of the approach embankment as far back from the river bank as possible.

"Trouble due to bad ground was by no means unknown in the neighbourhood; the east abutment of the old bridge had shown a similar tendency to lean towards the river, which was arrested by strengthening measures."

The Skelton Railway Bridge, otherwise known as Goole Railway Bridge.

The construction of the bridge at Keadby obviously took account of the needs of river traffic but its limitations in terms of road transport carrying capacity contributed to decisions to build a new motorway bridge at Burringham, which was part of a network leading to the Humber Bridge and the ports of Immingham and Grimsby.

It was also the rise of road traffic combined with the decline of river trade which led to an Act of Parliament in 1956 allowing the lifting section to be sealed in the down position.

An article in the Scunthorpe Telegraph two years later noted road improvement works had still not been carried out: "Despite strong opposition from shipping and river concerns and Gainsborough District Council an Act of Parliament authorised the 3,600 ton bridge's huge lifting span to become fixed in the down position from April 1, 1956."

The article also revealed alterations to give greater headroom to vehicles crossing the bridge and the moving of the pavement from inside the bridge to a cantilever footpath, enabling two lanes of traffic to cross the bridge.

Residents of Goole will be only too aware of the problems caused to river traffic by the listed railway bridge across the Ouse near Hook, for over the years numerous coasters have collided with it, in some cases affecting rail traffic, diverted via Selby. In this case the nearest road crossing is upstream at Boothferry Bridge.

Work on bridges can affect river passage, as illustrated by an information bulletin issued in relation to Goole Rail Bridge by British Waterways, covering October and November 2010: "Network Rail is undertaking refurbishment works to Goole Railway Bridge. Craft and plant will be present at the bridge for the duration of the works. One of the main navigable channels will remain open for the duration of the works. Updates can be obtained from the bridge control room on channel 9. The works and craft will be lit."

The Grade II* listed railway bridge, built in 1869, was designed by Thomas E Harrison and constructed by Butler and Pitts of Stanningley, with the swing section built by W G Armstrong and Co of Newcastle upon Tyne. The bridge was originally operated by hydraulic motors but now features electric motors. It was reported to be the second largest railway swing bridge in the world when it was built.

Another Grade II* listed bridge off the Humber is Horkstow Bridge over the River Ancholme near South Ferriby, previously mentioned.

The bridge replaced a ferry between Horkstow and Winterton and a riverside brickyard on the western bank. It is one of a few early suspension bridges in Britain which remains as it was designed. The deck was relaid in the 1990s by C Spencer Ltd, who won a commendation in the 1999 Institu-

One of the forts guarding the mouth of the Humber.

tion of Civil Engineers Historic Bridge Awards.

Apart from the fortifications at Paull, the most prominent ones on the Humber are the twin forts at its mouth between Spurn Point and Cleethorpes. Work on the two forts in the Humber, Haile and Bull, were started in 1914 to provide defences against enemy shipping. During the Second World War netting was strung across the estuary to prevent submarines making their way up the river.

The forts, with a diameter of 82ft, were constructed to provide accommodation for up to 200 servicemen.

Building Bull Fort was more problematic because the sandbank it stands on is 11ft below the surface at low water.

The forts were reported to have cost more than a £1-million to build and were regarded as a remarkable feat of engineering in their day. The Haile Sands Fort cost around £500,000 with Bull Fort costing twice that figure.

The two constructions saw no action in World War One and between the wars were not fully manned.

They were manned on the outbreak of the Second World War and according to local historian Alan Dowling, writing in the Cleethorpes Chronicle, their combined garrisons totalled 10 officers and 245 other ranks.

"Anti aircraft guns were installed and the forts saw much action against enemy aircraft and E-boats. An anti-submarine boom defence was also put across the mouth of the river.

The forts were vacated by the Army in 1956 and various ideas have been forwarded for their future use, including a drugs rehabilitation centre for Bull Fort.

Mr Dowling said the Humber provided the only suitable large-scale anchorage between the Thames and the River Forth and was of strategic importance to both the Royal Navy and Merchant shipping.

"The estuary also had some likely targets for enemy attack. On the south bank these included the Grimsby and Immingham docks, the Royal Navy's 35 oil tanks at Killingholme and the Admiralty wireless station at New Waltham – the principal wireless station on the east coast.

"So when war broke out in 1914, steps were taken to strengthen and extend the Humber defences. Gun batteries and other defence measures were constructed on both banks of the Humber."

Mr Dowling, who has penned books on both Cleethorpes and Grimsby, said: "Construction started in April, 1915. The contractors were C J Willis and son of London, whose operational base for the work was Grimsby.

"Building materials were ferried out from the Royal Dock but the operation's headquarters were at the extreme west end of Alexandra Dock."

Mr Dowling records: "A particular problem with Bull Sand Fort was that it was being built on sand which was 120ft deep. Work on the slightly smaller Haile Sand Fort progressed more speedily, partly because it was built on only a few feet of sand over clay and chalk."

Two four-inch guns were mounted on the Haile Sand Fort in April, 1917, and the fort was not officially completed until March, 1918. Bull Sand's four six-inch guns were put in place in March, 1918, with the fort completed in December, 1919.

Mr Dowling said the Bull Sand Fort was bought by the Humber Conservancy Board in 1964 for £625. In 1991 both forts were put up for sale by Associated British Ports for £50,000 each but made only £38,000.

Both forts went to auction in 1997 and according to Mr Dowling: "The Bull Sand Fort was purchased for £21,000 by the Basildon based charity Streetwise as a detox centre for drug addicts. Work is still being carried out to make the fort suitable for this purpose. The Haile Sand Fort was sold for £15,000 to a private English buyer.

Vessels on the old River Ancholme at Brigg with County Bridge to the rear.

Chapter 8: Remote Style of Life

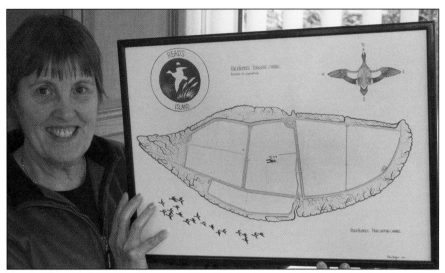

Dorothy Chapman in 2010, with a map of Read's Island presented to her on her departure. The map was penned by Miles Hopper, in 1973, when the island was much larger than it is today.

IMAGINE your worst fears, living on an island where the only neighbours are rats and mice. Such was the 'new life' that greeted Dorothy Chapman when she moved on to Read's Island in the River Humber in 1969.

It was to be her home for the next nine years and is now a rich vein of life's past conjuring up memories of adversity and isolation, which, mellowed by time, are now stripped of their pain with the humorous side being almost all that remains.

Dorothy, who hails from Nelson near Burnley, had been running a pub at Brinscall near Chorley, Lancashire, when her travelling engineer husband Roy Chapman, from Rothwell in northern Lincolnshire, heard the owners of the island were seeking a replacement gamekeeper.

Roy's father Harold Chapman had worked for the then owners, the Nickerson family, as a shepherd and had visited the island on a number of occasions.

The island was about twice the size it is nowadays and boasted a grass landing strip to the west, though access to the island for Dorothy and Roy was by shallow bottomed boats, the Mallard and later, the Curlew, which were moored in a muddy creek on the island, which lies just off Ferriby

Sluice on the south bank of the River Humber.

Today the island is a sanctuary for rare birds, including breeding avocets and some mistakenly refer to it as Reeds Island. However, the name comes from a Burton-upon-Stather farming family called Read, who reclaimed it from a sandbank.

The rats of the river had the run of the island and surrounding river banks but were somewhat larger than rats one might encounter at home.

Read's Island, off South Ferriby at low tide, about 40 years ago, with isle buildings top left and cement works top right. Image: Scunthorpe Telegraph archives.

"In our days on a clear day you could look towards Hessle and think you were seeing seals on the sand bank, but when you used binoculars you suddenly realised you were looking at rats," said Dorothy.

"Rats were everywhere on the island they used to pop up all over the shop. I do not like a dead rat never mind a live one. Roy used to say to me that if I did not touch them they would not touch me."

She said that prior to going on the island she had never really encountered rats but just didn't like them.

From her experience on the island she found they had generally come in for some bad press.

"I do not object to rats now. I have seen them in all situations. They are very clean animals and have gorgeous fur on them, she said.

"I do not think I was frightened of them, I just preferred not to encounter them."

Dorothy's late husband Roy Chapman

However, while on the island she recalled hunting for rat nests, which could often be spotted by a pyramid of material outside a smooth hold, indicating they had recently cleaned their nest out.

Dorothy would dig down and any rats that came out would be killed by her two dogs.

"On many a night when I got up at 3am to turn my duck eggs in the duck incubator,

She said she would see rats working their way through her vegetable patch, sampling the delights of her hard work, carrots, cabbage, a plant she knows as mercury, spinach and lettuce.

Dorothy said the nature of the silty mud soil meant there were many things they were not able to grow on the island.

Various factors led to the accretion of deposits. There have been suggestions it came from works on the River Ancholme, which services the market town of Brigg, and others that a wrecked ship created a barrier and led to the build up of deposits.

Local historian and retired fire officer Raymond Carey, in an account published by the River and John Frank Enterprises in aid of the Humber Keel and Sloop Preservation Society and the churches of South Ferriby and Horkstow, noted: "Ferriby Sands or Old Warp, from which the island was later to be made is first named in a 1734 navigation map."

He noted a large section of the river bank to the north of South Ferriby was washed away between 1830 and 1900, providing materials to enhance the existing sands.

"By 1820 much of the Old Warp was green topped, which was no doubt used for the summer grazing by enterprising farmers, but it was in the 1830s that the Read Brothers of Burton-upon-Stather must have realised the opportunities that the mud bank offered."

The discovery of a well on the island created the potential for settlement.

Sheep on Read's island with the house and shooting lodge.

Raymond Carey, with reference to the Read family, gives an outline of a process of regaining land from wetlands, used widely in the marshland valley off the River Humber.

"No doubt they were exponents of the techniques of winning land from the Trent called warping. A low wall is constructed during neap tides near the fringes or that area of the river to be claimed and the high spring tides are confined to allow the silt rich contents to settle, after which the water is released to the river at low tides. Many repeats of this left a very stable embanked island of rough soil."

The process meant that by 1836 there was an embanked island of about 40 acres and by then the family was employing a shepherd on the island. By 1841 the first map of the island showed it had been extended to about 80 acres and by 1906 measured 400 acres.

Because of concerns about the effect of the island on navigation the Humber Conservancy, which controlled navigation on the river, bought the land mass from the Crown for £9,000 in 1871 and by 1920 had established a magazine for the safe storage of explosives, used to remove wrecks from navigable channels.

Moving on to the island was a big change for Dorothy, then aged 27. She had enjoyed her time in the pub trade and earlier as a betting shop manageress.

It was a bleak rainy day and she recalled questioning what she had let herself in for, especially when she saw how dirty the house, which had not been used for years, had become.

"The house was filthy, there was no water, and no electricity. The generator did not work and there was no diesel for the generator. When we got some diesel we had a job to get the generator working."

As fuel for heating for the property, for the fire and the cooker she used

Read's Island in 2008 with South Ferriby cement works across the water.

Read's Island across the South Channel, looking in the direction of Brough. The island has now been abandoned to the birds, attracting rare breeds like avocets.

driftwood with the weekly chore of traipsing round the island picking up suitable wood which had been washed up on the shores.

Calor gas was also available on the island for cooking and to cool the couple's fridge, which by modern standards was miniscule, excess items relying on a traditional larder.

Like the neighbouring shooting lodge, the house was raised up from the general ground level. It had a sitting room and two utility rooms, with two upstairs bedrooms.

The shooting lodge had two bedrooms, a kitchen and pantry, but no bathroom and visitors had to use the facilities in the house.

The house was in the centre of the island surrounded by 200 acres of grassland and a further 250 acres of marshland.

Roy, who died of cancer in 1986, was employed as a gamekeeper, shepherd and general handyman with Dorothy as the cook for shooting parties, organised by the Nickerson estate of Rothwell, from September through to January. They were shooting wildfowl and ducks.

The couple, who had a small black and white television, were not totally isolated and subject to the tides Dorothy found time to do some book keeping for Joe Coral's in Scunthorpe and bar shifts at the Hope and Anchor at Ferriby Sluice.

Shooting back and forth was not always plain sailing and on one occasion Dorothy and Roy nearly perished while trying to cross the south channel on their way to South Ferriby.

In the murky morning mist there came a loud shout and then suddenly the large Norwegian car carrier of the Ugland Management Co (Hoegh-Ugland Auto Liners), possibly the Autostrada, emerged towering over them. Roy manoeuvred their tiny Mallard just in time and they breathed a sigh of relief.

"You do not realise how frightening it was. We ended up on the mud banks just outside South Ferriby Sluice," said Dorothy.

She said maintaining boat access to the island was an ever pressing need. The main creek for landing on the island used by the couple was from the South Ferriby end. The creek led to a sluice gate with a mini harbour ahead of it. To the west were the Home Fields around the house.

In the area close to the landing creek was a system of drainage dykes which enabled a flushing of the creek to help keep it open.

She said that when the tide came in the sluice gate was opened and the water would wash through the creek to swill the channel and wash away rubbish. When the tide was low the sluice gate was opened and the water washed through the creek to swill the channel. Despite the sluicing there remained about three feet of cloying mud at the bottom of the channel.

Dorothy said the Neap tides were 22ft to 23ft but the spring tides could be between 25ft and 30ft, affecting the accessibility for boats to the island.

Although Roy had built makeshift jetties to enable easier access to the

The house and lodge top left of this view of Read's Island with the muddy inlet cum harbour, where vessels could land at high tide, at the bottom of the photo.

The house on the left and the shooting lodge on the right.

firm land, on one occasion, while transporting a new mattress to the island they came unstuck. The mattress arrived too late for the tide to take the delivering boat fully up the creek. They chose to beach the boat and then transfer the mattress overboard with Dorothy dropping on to the muddy shore to pull it on to firmer land.

"As soon as I jumped over the boat I was in slurry. I had to kick my waders off. I took my jeans off and I got up to the dryer part of the slurry."

She worked her way up the mire on her bottom, leaving her jeans and waders behind and made her way to the house in her knickers and with no shoes. Fortunately the mattress, which had been wrapped in polythene, survived the ordeal.

While on the island the couple had two dogs, a springer-spaniel cross called Whisky and a border collie called Pip. They helped round up the sheep on the island but they were not properly trained sheepdogs.

There was a fence surrounding the immediate area of the house to ensure the animals could not get right up to it, but this obviously did not apply to the rats, the dominant wildlife, far outnumbering the occasional rabbit.

Both of the pet dogs were seasoned rat catchers but sheer number of rats on the island encouraged Dorothy to keep the windows and doors to the house closed whenever possible.

"I came back one day and there was a rat in the pantry," she said.

On disturbing the rat it scurried away escaping the tin of beans she had hurled at it, with a view to a kill rather than encouraging the creature to become a flatulent rat. With the help of the dogs it was eventually tracked down and caught, but the episode took a full hour.

Dorothy recalled the rats being active early in the day: "Rats came and played in the garden and you could watch them in the morning."

She said the sheep were put on the island soon after they arrived and they had the duty of having to count them every day. There were around 28 sheep, which were free to roam and while most stayed in the grassland area occasionally one would go astray and be found in one of the island inlets.

"The sheep were a pain, they never did anything you wanted them to," said Dorothy

A herd of deer were taken to the island in 1976 on an engineless barge which was strapped alongside the island boat the Mallard. The couple also cared for two donkeys which were pets of the Nickerson family.

The deer proved more problematic than the sheep, especially in the rutting season, when one made a noise like a foghorn in the early hours of the morning while raking his antlers and a fence.

While the deer may have caused some anguish, the birdlife brightened up Dorothy's life and she became something of a twitcher, noting short-eared owls, curlew, lapwings, bullfinches, shell ducks and widgeon.

While there were taps in the house, the water was not on a mains system and the couple had to pump water from a natural spring on the island to top up the tank in the house. The water was mere multi-purpose water unfit to drink. The drinking water was brought from South Ferriby each day in two five gallon containers.

Another onerous task faced by the couple was emptying their own septic tank, separating out the solids and then burying them. In Dorothy's eyes the tank was a little closer to the house than she would have chosen to put it.

However, she has one amusing tale from when a couple of friends, John and Edna Woods, came to visit the island. During his time there John was not very well and had been sick down the toilet. Unfortunately his false teeth had also gone down the pot.

Equipped with boiled water and a couple of ladles, the wooden cover to the cesspit was freed and the set of teeth fished out by Dorothy. The teeth were cleaned on the island and later sent off by John's dentist for sterilising. On a later visit Dorothy asked John whether he was wearing the 'cesspit' pair of teeth, but for some reason never got a straight forward answer.

In recent years her experiences of life on the island have been the subject of talks she gives to a variety of organisations across northern Lincolnshire.

The talks started by accident. Dorothy was a member of the St Bartholemew's Church Women's Guild at Keelby, when at one meeting the booked speaker failed to materialise. Someone said they could have a quiz but then Dorothy volunteered to speak about her time on the island. Over the years the life with the rats has interested listeners.

"They find the fact you have to live with rats most fascinating," said Dorothy.

She said for many people, because they did not see a rat they felt there were none about, when in actual fact they were quite common.

Dorothy (right) and a friend on Read's island.

In addition to the farmers and gamekeepers on the island, who built up the defensive banks as part of their duties, it is believed working parties enhanced them during the Crimean War period and also during the First World War when German prisoners of war were engaged on the project.

In addition to bits of wood and a regular supply of Grimsby fish baskets washed up on shore there was a most unusual form of 'rain' back in the summer of 1974, when pieces of insulation and aluminium rained down and were washed up on the island. It was debris from the massive chemical plant explosion at Flixborough, on the nearby River Trent, in which 28 people lost their lives.

Winteringham Parish and Census records note that in the early days the island was only occupied on a seasonal basis but records in South Ferriby mention a Selena Osgerby was born there. The village school log notes a number of children living on the island over a number of years, their attendance being typified by occasional lateness due to the varying tides.

In the 1861 census shepherd William Foster of Crosby, Scunthorpe and his wife and two children were noted as being on the island, while by 1871 John Hewitt and five children, aged one to nine were living there.

A tenant called Mr Dougherty in 1888, the year the Football League was founded, is noted as paying £650 in rent for use of a wooden cottage and farm buildings. By 1892 the land was let by R and H C Ford for £520, the previous tenant being moved from the island for what was described as bad husbandry, which presumably related to failing to maintain protective banks on the north side of the island.

The Kirkby family farmed the island for a number of years around 1900.

Dorothy recalled having seen Bill Kirkby, a member of the family which farmed the island, in Barton-upon-Humber, in recent years.

In 1951, aged 11, Archie Campbell recalled moving to the island with his brother and mother and father. According to excerpts from an article reproduced by village historian Raymond Carey, Archie noted: "Spring there was beautiful, with hundreds of birds nesting everywhere; pewits, greenshanks and red-shanks, larks, coots, mallards and teals. Curlew were there too but I never found their nests. With hundreds of cattle grazing at this time of the year, it always amazed me that so few nests were trampled on.

"I ran free from April to September; my mother, being a teacher, looked after my needs until the summer holiday when I sat the 11 plus and went to Barton-upon-Humber Grammar School, to finish my education. This meant going into lodgings on the mainland."

He was often taken back to the island on a weekend by his school pal David Mouncey, who in later years worked for the Environment Agency near the island and was a prominent member of the Humber Yawl Club, the south section of which is based at nearby Winteringham.

Archie said: "Sometimes in the summer my school pal David Mouncey would take me home on Friday evenings. We'd scull across in a 'coggie' and I would walk up the mud bank to dry land and home again before the next tide."

In 1953 the Scunthorpe Evening Telegraph noted Mr and Mrs Duncan Campbell lived on the island with their son, who was named as Sandy, aged 18. Mrs Campbell had been a schoolteacher and had an MA from Glasgow University.

In an old clipping she was quoted as saying: "We spend the evenings reading or listening to the radio. We rarely bother to go ashore."

The article noted Mr Campbell was charged with looking after 300 head of cattle.

Way back then Mr Campbell noted receding mud banks, in his opinion, combined with low flying aircraft, had reduced the number of geese in the area of the island.

He said shooting on the island was confined to once a fortnight.

A further clipping from the Telegraph's Wayfarer column in August 1954 noted the family had used a one time assault craft for crossing between the mainland and island. The craft was named Pinkfoot.

The article noted the island was leased from the Humber Conservancy Board by F R Davy of Louth and Mr J Nickerson of Rothwell.

The lease for the island was put up for sale in 1969 but only attracted bids of £32,000 when £50,000 was hoped for.

The island was featured on the BBC Northern Home Service in the programme North Countryman in January 1959 when it was occupied by the Forester family, including a son and two daughters.

In 1965 the island was occupied by the Swan family, with James, aged nine, attending South Ferriby School. The farmhouse had a two way radio with Nickerson's head office at Cherry Valley Farm, Rothwell. Scotsman William Donner, a farm hand, was also noted as helping on the island.

On September 11, 1987, the local paper noted the latter days of Read's island as a habitable farmstead with dramatic news of flooding on the island.

"The couple living on Read's island in the River Humber, abandoned their home this morning as the high tides breached an emer-

Mr R Kirkby, with Mr Kirkby Snr. and Nap, at the shooting Lodge on Read's Island. Picture from the Smith Collection at David Lee Photography.

gency flood bank and virtually covered the island.

"Les Burbidge and his wife Jenny had been warned to expect the worst and evacuated the island when all but 30 acres was covered around 10am.

"Their 100-year-farmhouse was safe on top of a slight hill and a small herd of fallow deer were said to be safe and grazing peacefully."

However, it was understood the well on the island had been contaminated.

"The marathon battle to plug a 10 metre gap in the main flood bank began yesterday after an exceptionally high tide had burst through, virtually submerging the island under 3ft of water."

Dorothy, who was born in August 1942, said she recalled Roy constructing an additional bank on the eastern tip of the north side of the island, which along with other defences did their job while they were on the island.

"All the time I lived on Read's Island, the water never breached the banks," she said.

Following their spell on the island, Roy sadly died from cancer and Dorothy went to work for the Grimsby Fish merchants Richard Coulbeck Ltd, being employed in the office and becoming company secretary.

"I worked there for 12 years until 2000 and then two or three years with CCS Fish. I then became semi-retired," she said.

The island today is jointly managed by the RSPB and the Lincolnshire Wildlife Trust on lease from the Joseph Nickerson Trust. With the co-operation of the Environment Agency, two large lagoons have been created on the island which provide a suitable habitat for avocets, black headed gulls, redshanks and lapwing.

In 2004, the then warden of Blacktoft Sands, which had responsibility for Read's Island, Peter Short, said the banking on the island, which had been maintained and built up while it was inhabited, was no longer a viable means of protection. With rising tides predicted the island could in future years return to what it had been before it was embanked.

Mr Short recorded the creek by the sluice gate on the south side of the island had silted up and access was via the north side and was particularly dangerous given the crumbling cliffs and the main shipping channel.

"You have to land commando style against 15ft of crumbling cliff and you have a chance of going up to your waist in mud."

He said the rip of the tide at that point was apparently the fastest on the Yorkshire and Humberside Coast.

He concluded: "It will never be a habitable island again because of the changes in economics and the changes in sea levels."

With changing tidal flows in the River Humber, Dorothy disagreed with

It certainly was a case of, The End is Nigh, when high tides and storms hit the island in the 1980s. The current island is only half the size it was and with watery beds designed to attract birds it is hard to believe anyone ever lived there.

Mr and Mrs Duncan Campbell, around 1953, at the door of their Read's Island home. Their son Sandy also lived with them. Mr Campbell looked after the 300 head of cattle which had what was described as excellent grazing on the island's 400 acres.

the suggestion it might never be habitable again.

She herself would not wish to return, but that is not through the fact half the island has gone and the cottage and shooting lodge have been demolished, but more of a personal nature.

"Somebody asked would I ever go back, but I do not think so because I think it would upset me too much. You think about what you lost. I think it would bring back sad memories of Roy."

The landing craft for Read's Island was repaired by the Clapson family, which for generations had a boatyard at Barton but as the traditional barge craft water trade waned, opened a chandlery, mainly for pleasure craft at South Ferriby in 1967, later adding a workshop and repair facilities.

Rodney Clapson, said: "Read's Island was tenanted and when I first knew the people there they had a converted landing craft which we did repairs on."

"The craft was used for cattle to run out of."

Mr Clapson said they later used pontoons to carry the livestock, which were towed out to the island.

He said in his day the cattle had gone from the island. It was by then occupied by sheep. They were carried across the river from the area of Low Farm, upriver from Ferriby Sluice, where the road is close to the river. It wasn't practical to use the jetties to transfer them.

The isolation of people living on the island was viewed as something of an endurance test. Rodney said it was a hard life. All they had to go out on was a 25ft boat.

He said the mud was a problem for those on the island and he was told a tale by a doctor from Winterton who had to go out to the island when a woman on it was pregnant. He said he had to make his way through cloying mud and even when he reached the house there was mud everywhere, even on the woman's bed.

"In those days the island was a lot bigger. All the north side has gone and ABP made them pull the house down. They did not want lengths of timber to go into the water and get into any propellors."

While still clinging resolutely to the seaward tip of the East Riding, Spurn Point has and still is intermittently an island whose long term future as part of the mainland is most certainly in doubt.

Like Read's Island upriver it is a remote place for families living there but today is in many ways more connected than in years gone by.

Reads Island has shrunk with the movement of channels in the river but the Spurn sand spit is now being breached with some degree of regularity.

Superintendent Coxwain of the RNLI Humber Lifeboat Station, Dave Steenvoorden, where The Pride of the Humber is stationed with a full time

The modern day lifeboat at Spurn, Pride of the Humber.

Spurn lifeboatmen from the early 20th century.

crew, said the peninsula road was now experiencing 'constant washovers' at high tides without there being bad weather.

"If we feel there is a danger of it being washed over we move all the cars over to the top end," he said.

Breaching of the road is not a new thing but serious bad weather could cut access and make life for the lifeboat community at the point even more isolated than it is today.

The prevailing tides along the East Coast are from the North to the South, which has led to the creation of the spit through the gnawing away of the Holderness coastline with the loss of several villages and in due course a one time major port of Ravenspur, at the mouth of the Humber before the spit crept inland.

The spit was breached at Chalk Bank in 1849, creating a rift of 1,500ft by 16ft. The gap was not sealed until 1855 at a cost of £25,000, a huge sum in those days.

The stretch of the spit, known as Narrow Neck, was breached in 1856, leaving a gaping gap 240ft wide and 13ft deep at high tide.

If one takes a stroll or drive down the road from Kilnsea the constant erosion is self evident with stretches of one time road having collapsed or gaily tossed onto the eastward beach by the forces of nature.

Beach scattered pill boxes also note the march of erosion and also signal the importance of the spit as a military site in past conflicts, seeing it fortified in the Napoleonic era, the First World War and the Second World War.

There was once a railway between the point and Kilnsea, which boasts a concrete 'sound mirror' to give early warning of approaching Zeppelins during the First World War. Goods and equipment were taken down to the point on railway bogeys fitted with a mast and sails to utilise wind power.

The government chose to abolish the coastal defence artillery in 1956 and the spit passed into the hands of the Yorkshire Naturalists Trust which later became the Yorkshire Wildlife Trust. The main presence on the peninsula is the lifeboatmen, pilots for the Humber, nature reserve personnel, birdwatchers and inquisitive tourists seeking out tranquillity.

In the year 2010 the lifeboatmen marked the 200th anniversary of the staging of a lifeboat on the peninsula by Hull Trinity House, which in those

Spurn lifeboatmen from the early 20th century. Photos: Courtesy RNLI.

days was the authority responsible for navigation of the river.

The first lifeboat was a rowing boat manned by 10 men who travelled from Kilnsea before manhandling their vessel into the sea. By 1819 cottages had been built by Trinity House of Hull and some rights, such as loading vessels with sand and fishing, were bestowed upon the lifeboatmen.

The RNLI took over the running of the station in 1911 and while life there has always been isolated, with modern technology it is less remote than it once was.

Like many riverside families, incursions of water into their homes was simply part of a way of life with washboards against doorways used in often vain attempts to stop interior flooding.

While the point was isolated there was a constant flow of seamen willing to buy vegetables tended by the lifeboatmen and in the early 20th century there were regular visits by boat from visitors to Cleethorpes across the river.

Mr Steenvoorden, who originates from Cleethorpes, said the Severn Class The Pride of the Humber worked in tandem with the smaller D-Class Blue Peter VI at Cleethorpes. They also worked closely with the Hessle based Humber Rescue, a separate charity, which dealt with many incidents further up the river.

At the time of writing the rescue services were due to be enhanced by the addition of an intermediate sized Atlantic 85 vessel at Cleethorpes, which

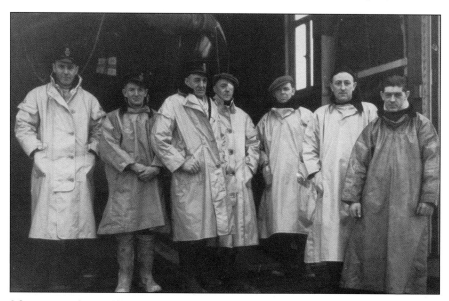

A Spurn crew with the lifeboat to the rear.

A view of Spurn from an old souvenir card. Note the washing and allotments.

has been sanctioned by the RNLI but was awaiting suitable housing.

Living on Spurn point requires a special kind of person who can cope with the isolation, the nearest pub being an eight mile round trip to Kilnsea, the nearest primary school and paper shop is at Easington, requiring a 16 mile round trip while the nearest senior school is in Withernsea, entailing a 30 mile round trip with two buses from Kilnsea and a drive up the spit from the point.

Mr Steenvoorden said adapting to the remoteness of life on Spurn was the hardest thing for families to crack when moving there and lifeboatmen who left did so for their families or to further their careers.

A more recent view of the Spurn settlement with two lighthouses.

"The problem is you cannot go to the shop every day, you have to look at a week or a month in advance," he said.

However, he added shopping was being made easier by the delivery service of some shops and a recently enhanced internet link-up with the mainland.

With numerous visitors in the summer residents, experience the opposite of being cut off from society.

"You need to be a tolerant person; you are living in a goldfish bowl and you need the backing of your family."

He said the turnover of crew was fairly stable but the ones who didn't last normally went because the families could not cope with the distance from anywhere.

Mr Steenvoorden, aged 53 and a former fisherman, said living on the station remained remote but things were not as they were in the 1800s because of things like the internet.

The remoteness did, however, help to promote a real community which now probably only remained in rural villages.

"We have the most fantastic bonfires and birthdays and families pull together; if one of the wives is ill the rest of the crew cover for them."

He said the men did five days on duty and were not allowed to leave the

Not quite the modern car, this contraption was used on the miniature railway to carry goods.

Forget about global warming, people around the Humber have been using wind power for years as this bogie on the way to Spurn Point illustrates.

base. They then had a day off before working a further five days on a rolling roster which gave them one weekend off in seven. There were no Bank Holidays.

"I believe I am doing the best job in England. I am doing something I passionately believe in," said Dave, who has been on Spurn for over 10 years and is due to retire in 2012.

He said the station averaged 53 plus jobs a year, covering one of England's main arteries in terms of shipping tonnage and massive ships putting into North Killingholme, Hull, Immingham and Grimsby.

Mr Steenvoorden said 65 per cent of call-outs were to commercial shipping with around five per cent devoted to searches.

He said Hull was the nearest hospital by land and a Land Rover was fitted out with first-aid equipment to ferry people from the point to meet an ambulance at Kilnsea, though any water bound injuries from boats were

A view down the neck of Spurn shows how vulnerable it is to the sea.

taken to Grimsby and the Diana, Princess of Wales hospital on the south bank. In some circumstances a helicopter was used to take injured people to hospital.

The loneliness of Spurn was noted in a booklet by George A Jarratt, produced from his notes by the lifeboat station, featuring memories of Spurn in the 1880s, penned by the author in 1956. He said it was like a city compared with his childhood there in the 1880s when there were just 10 lifeboat cottages, homes for three lighthouse keepers in the circular base yard of a former lighthouse and the old Lifeboat Inn where the crews of wrecked ships were cared for.

The Coxwain of the Humber lifeboat from 1810 to 18 41 was Robert Richardson, who also ran the Lifeboat Inn.

He said there were two lighthouses in operation, the High Light, which threw a beam out into the North Sea, and the Low Light which stood in the Humber and threw a beam on to the River Humber.

Mr Jarratt noted they would travel further afield by train from Partrington railway station, via a boat to Kilnsea, a walk to Easington and a ride on an open waggonette to Partrington. The only alternative was to walk 15 miles.

The only 'land bound' people they saw regularly were the postman and a preacher from Patrington Primitive Methodist Circuit, who would ride by trap to Kilnsea and walk the rest of the way before conducting a service in an upper room of the lighthouse. Sunday School general schooling was in the Coxwain's house with the same room being the telegraph station and post office.

The isolation of the community is brought home by one quote: "We children did not know the worth of money, there being no shops nearer than eight miles away. We could get a few boiled sweets when one of the boats sailed across to Grimsby, taking their crabs to market there. They used to take a sailor bag and a list from each housewife, of groceries they needed and brought them back."

More so than the lifeboat community today, the families had to plan ahead and fend for themselves. The main meat was rolled sides of bacon. They also had home grown potatoes reared in sand and seaweed, Hornsea Herring apples and flour. Some members of the community kept a few hens and a pig, quite usual in those days in both towns and villages.

The lifeboat folk ate wild rabbits, blackbird, starlings and rooks and the occasional wild duck. There were also the fruits of the sea and occasional bags of ships biscuits.

Water was mainly rainwater and barrels shipped in by Trinity House during the dry season. Milk was tinned.

Heating was provided by driftwood and sea washed coal with lighting provided by candle. When the men went out on a rescue the women and children knew they were all by themselves bar the lighthousemen who were on duty.

Mr Jarratt noted Trinity House would not provide a school or teacher for children on the point, which meant they were less well educated compared with their counterparts on the mainland..

He recalled the occasion his own family and others moved off Spurn.

"What an upheaval there was in the days before we left the Point, when the five families had to be moved. Sloops came up at high water in front of the cottages at the Humber side and when the tide receded, the goods were packed into the holds, when the tide rose again, they sailed away to Hull."

The incident showed the versatility of the flat bottomed vessels with groundings rarely due to error, more frequently to design.

The binks or banks on the seaward side of Spurn Point were frequently visited by sanders and gravellers, who would set themselves down as one tide ebbed and spend the intervening hours loading up with sand or gravel, ready to be floated off by the next incoming tide.

Debris from Spurn was used for road and other building projects with keels and sloops delivering the materials as far as Brough, South Ferriby and beyond. Materials from Spurn were also reputedly used in the construction of Immingham Dock, which opened on July 22, 1912, with the Humber ferry boat the Killingholme carrying royalty to the event.

The sand/gravel was also used as ballast in seagoing vessels but the 'run on sand' led to the Humber Conservancy (which controlled the river) requiring licenses for its commercial extraction off Spurn.

In the early 1800s the stretch of land was in the hands of the Constable family which with the agreement of Trinity House gave the lifeboatmen of the peninsula preference in the loading of sloops with sand and gravel, enabling them to earn £80 a year but as water replaced sand and gravel as ballast the income which helped support their meagre existence gradually reduced. At one stage according to Trinity House records, there were 500 vessels visiting the peninsula for sand and gravel.

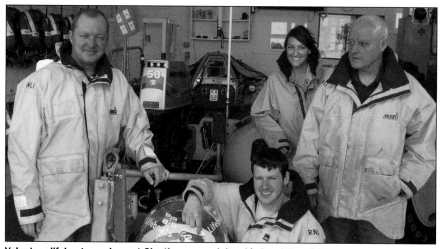

Volunteer lifeboat members at Cleethorpes work hand in hand the with men on the north bank.

The first floating lightship was reportedly Betsy who was put off Spurn in 1820 after being hired from William Walker of Grimsby. The first permanent lightship was installed in 1832. Up until 1905 all lights were fixed, later boasting cycles of flashes.

Chapter 9: Disasters and treasures

WE have already referred to old vessels being found in the swampland areas of the River Humber and there are wrecks a plenty to be found along the estuary and beyond its mouth.

With all the shoals and the changing tides the River Humber has been described as one of the most dangerous in England and more than one or two have come a cropper, though in many cases the wrecks of vessels are long gone washed away by the tide.

Scattered around the mouth of the Humber along the line of Spurn sand spit many wooden vessels met their deaths but there were also disasters further upstream. Isabel Sanderson (nee Bray) was brought up in the village of Whitton close to the confluence of the Rivers Trent and Ouse.

In a short history of her early days she recalls: "We were given countless warnings of the dangers which lurked in and near the river and told particularly, that we must never ever, venture out on to the great sandbanks which were revealed at low tide, however inviting the long stretches of wave patterned golden sand might be.

"There were patches of quicksand, we were told and thousands of tons were liable to move at any time."

Mrs Sanderson recalled they were told: "You will hear a noise like thunder and the sand will shift and sink and you will be swallowed up and never be seen again."

The river posed obvious dangers for adventurous children but also for their parents sailing upon it, from a jetty which once stretched out into the turbulent waters and connected the community through steam packets to the likes of Hull and Gainsborough.

So dangerous was this stretch of the river that should Mrs Sanderson said there was an old jingle recited in the village: "Between Trent Falls and Whitton Ness many are made widow and fatherless."

She recorded: "The Ness was a promontory jutting out into the river about a quarter of a mile downstream from the village, and an unmanned lightship was anchored a few hundred yards out from the shore at that point to warn shipping of the deadly dangerous sandbanks, undercurrents and invisible shadows and deeps.

The Lightships, she said, were known as Whitton One and Whitton Two and were anchored out in the river right opposite the church.

"We often saw the light of Whitton Two as we went home on Sundays after Evensong. In rough weather the light tossed up and down and the lightship's bell, deep toned, resonant, rang out loud and clear above the roar of the wind and the noise of the wild turbulent waves."

One of the Whitton lightships, the Audrey, was restored and converted into a sailing pleasure craft giving youngsters experience of the river before passing into private hands. For some years it was in Humber Dock but more recently has moved south to the River Thames. As well as unmanned lightships there were manned vessels with crew areas.

The lightship Audrey was built by Joshua Watson of Gainsborough in 1915, being one of three vessels marking the sandbanks around Whitton. She was built for the Humber Conservancy Board.

The vessel was bought by the Goole Sobriety project in 1986 and in 1998 underwent a £75,000 refurbishment at Beverley, being converted into a gaff rigged ketch Goole Billy Boy. She is 60ft long and 17ft 6ins wide.

The dangerous waters off Whitton claimed the Norwegian Ship Neptun J Laurentzen in the 1930s but in this instance the crew of the vessel were fortunately saved.

Jessie Grant (nee Burgess) who was brought up in Whitton alongside the River Humber, close to where the old jetty stood, recalled the sinking of the Norwegian Ship in a newspaper article in July 2007.

She apparently accompanied her father Henry Stacey Burgess, out on to the river in a small motor boat, along with her brother Ivor Burgess and sister Yvonne Burgess.

"They hailed us from the boat that was sinking, " she recounted.

Mrs Grant said she recalled seeing the crew on board the coal carrying ship. What particularly stood out was the image of the Norwegian seamen eating raw eggs.

Her father had been taking the family to South Ferriby, but put herself and her brother and sister on a red lightship so he could aid the seamen. Back then lightships were manned around the clock by two men employed by the Humber Conservancy, which controlled navigation on the river.

The seamen were put ashore but her father found someone had stood on the engine mechanism and he was forced to row the boat back to Whitton with her sister at the rudder.

The pier at Whitton was completed in 1865 with vessels calling at the village previously docking at a rough stone landing 400 yards upstream. The new structure featured a stone jetty which sloped down to the water and a wooden pier of 200ft with a stroke across the end for a T shaped jetty providing a berth for steam packets. The pier was removed in 1920 and since 1910 the village was connected to the outside world by the North

A sinking ship, opposite Whitton School, in 1934 thought to be the Norwegian coal carrier. The sands of Whitton were known as a very dangerous place.

Lindsey Light Railway from which passenger services ended in 1925, though freight continued to 1951.

Details about shipwrecks in the lower reaches of the River Humber and the surrounding coast have recently been the subject of a research programme by a group of diving enthusiasts aided by a grant from the Heritage Lottery Fund.

The shipwrecks of the River Humber group was charged with pinpointing the location of wrecks and providing additional information. It was also to make accounts of the life of the vessel, its building, its working life, its benefit and involvement with the local community and its loss to the community when it sank.

Cleethorpes born group spokesman Kevin Smith said: "We need to record these events for all and keep these records for the future generations to show how the area has evolved."

"Like family history you dig for details but not all wrecks are named and on the North East coast only 20 per cent are identified," he said.

The lower reaches of the River Humber are not only very murky but are fast flowing and dangerous to work in. Many of the wrecked ships in the area have deliberately been blown up to ensure they pose no risk to current day shipping.

The grant given to the group was £24,500 and provided money for a boat, side sonar equipment, underwater cameras and printing. The team concentrated on researching wrecks in a 20 mile circuit around the mouth of the estuary.

"We have taken a lot of underwater video, sonar images and sketches of wrecks on a database of 600 to 700 wrecks, based on various agencies which had records in the past," said Kevin.

Their quest was assisted in 2007 by the Royal Navy vessel HMS Gleaner, which visited the Humber to map details of wrecks for the Admiralty and gave access to some of its work to the group.

Kevin said that in times of conflict enemy vessels would often position themselves next to wrecks to give themselves cover because defending forces would be hoodwinked into thinking they were the wrecked ship.

Kevin Smith pores over his charts.

Hence, the more information available to the Admiralty the more able they were to identify enemy vessels.

The research group was assisted by Grimsby and Cleethorpes Sub-Aqua Club, including Kevin of Scartho, as chairman, Bob Eagle of Grimsby as treasurer, Billy Hill of Saltfleetby as diving operations manager and Martin Fry of Cleethorpes. Underwater images were taken by Pete Wardle and John Leslie, both of Grimsby.

Kevin estimated there were about 50 wrecks in the mouth of the River Humber including everything from Grimsby and Hull trawlers to seine netters and merchant ships from all over the world.

The 600 to 700 wrecks plotted and recorded in the survey were only the tip of the iceberg, with lost vessels not finding their way into the record books because they were not recorded at the time of the shipwreck.

He said this was understandable when on some nights in centuries past there were reports of more than 100 vessels being lost on the Lincolnshire coast.

He said on the Stony Binks just beyond Spurn, where the southerly coastal currents tussled with the outbound currents of the Humber, the remains of many wooden vessels wrecked upon the shores had been obliterated over the years. It was also worth noting the coast in past centuries was further out into the North Sea than it is today.

He said trawlermen from Grimsby and other fishermen had been able to give valuable snippets of information relating to the position of wrecks and details relating to circumstances and seamen on the vessels. In many cases the details came to light when they had snagged their fishing nets on something beneath the water and recorded the details to stop a similar thing happening in the future.

The most distant wreck the

A diver connected with the shipwrecks of the river Humber group searches for remains of a wreck off the Humber Coast in the North Sea.

team looked at was that of the Benmacdhui, which is about 18 miles north east of Spurn, 25 metres down, in two pieces, after being sunk by a German aircraft in 1941.

Kevin said the ship had been heading to visit the British Expeditionary forces in the Far East and boasted a cargo akin to whatever one could buy in Binns or Debenhams at the time.

The wreck had been bought by Eddie Kirkpatrick of Hull who had salvaged several thousand pounds of brass and bronze, though he allowed the divers to visit the wreck.

Kevin said when diving anything one found had to be reported to the Maritime and Coastal Agency's Receiver of Wrecks in Southampton.

"After you find the item and if they cannot find the owner, then after a year and a day it is yours to keep."

He said many owners of wrecks were happy with divers taking souvenirs as proper salvage equipment was needed to raise quantities of valuable heavy metals to the surface.

"People in our club have had ammunition – empty shell cases – there are tons of ordnance on some wrecks, we do not touch that."

Speaking of the Benmacdhui he said: "There are golf balls, spoons, knives and forks, Pond's cold cream, Brylcream, Marmite, scent bottles, cement bags set solid, big rolls of film, Yale padlocks, cycle parts, truck tyres, railway parts, everything you could buy, it is like an Aladdin's cave.

"We bring back bits and pieces like silver tongs and portholes; we do not go out there plundering wrecks.

"People have a perception there is this ship sat there but it is like a shipwreck scrapyard. They have been blown apart when they went down or the Navy has dispersed them. Once you are over 35 to 40 metres down they are not a danger to shipping so they are more or less left as they were when they went down."

However, he pointed out that banks of sand in the river mouth and out to sea changed as currents varied so parts of a wreck could surface one year but be hidden the next.

The iron steamship Marshall was ferrying immigrants from Germany to Hull for transfer to Liverpool and across the Atlantic, to a new life in America, when she went down on November 28, 1853.

Kevin said the Marshall was in collision with a barque called Woodhouse, at night in thick fog, a little over six miles out of the Humber. The Woodhouse survived but the 60 crew and immigrants on the Marshall were lost.

Another collision off the River Humber involved the English iron steamship Homer on February 15, 1901, 20 miles out from the mouth of the River Humber and a Russian barque, the wreckage now lying 26 metres underwater.

Some of the natural treasures under the sea.

The Homer had been sailing between London and Newcastle while the Russian ship was bound for the USA.

Kevin said records noted that on the point of impact an English seaman called McAllister jumped aboard the Russian ship and the Russian captain jumped aboard the English ship. All those on board the Russian ship, including McAllister, survived, while all on the other vessel perished.

Another wreck off the mouth of the Humber is that of the Speedwell, 10 miles south east of Spurn, which was in collision with another ship in 1868 while carrying pottery to Swansea.

"It was a schooner made of wood which was built in 1802. There were two survivors. I found it was owned by Captain Dyl Wyn who was also the master," said Kevin.

Kevin said the boat was Dyl Wyn's whole life, containing all his assets. The crockery found on the vessel was stamped with Swansea Pottery but on contact with a museum in South Wales he found their records showed the pottery had ceased production in the 1840s and what appeared to be happening was 'counterfeit' pottery from Newcastle was being shipped to America where it was passed off as the genuine high quality Swansea Pottery.

Around eight miles out of the Humber near Haile Sands buoy, are the remains of the City of Birmingham, which hit a mine in 1940, during the Second World War, while en route from Beira to Hull.

The 5,300 gross tonnage City of Birmingham was carrying copper, copper ingots, tin, ammunition, wool, tea and tobacco. In the late 1940s a salvage company, Risdon Beazley, had recovered copper and tin from the wreck worth £2-million.

Kevin said they used to dive quite often near the City of Birmingham but a change to the routeing of traffic had reduced the possibilities of dives there.

The wreck of the ship Canada is still marked by a buoy 13 miles north of Spurn Point, two miles offshore. The ship left Hull on November 3, 1939 and just north of Spurn was holed when she struck a mine off Withernsea.

The incident is recorded on a group leaflet: "Everybody on board left the ship in the lifeboats, but as the vessel was apparently not sinking, the Captain, together with 12 crew, went back on board.

"The remaining part of the crew and all passengers were taken up by another ship passing by and subsequently landed at Grimsby.

As it was still possible to run the main engine, the course was set towards the shore. The vessel was put aground about 10 nautical miles from the Humber lightship due east of Humberston.

"The remaining cargo consisted of soya beans in bags and even though the crew tried to pump the damaged holds dry, the entering water made the Soya beans expand to an extent, which made the hull burst and caused a total destruction of the vessel.

"A few days later the Greek steamer Georgios collided with the wreck and was stuck on the foredeck .

Some of the disasters on the rivers were not seen as much more than just part of life as was alluded to by the reference to the jingle about Whitton Sands, mentioned earlier.

Before the channelling of the outfall of the Trent and Ouse sand banks were frequently moving and it was not always possible for even the most seasoned of sailor to predict anything other than in certain weather and with certain tidal and other conditions it was dangerous.

Before the coming of engines rivermen tended to describe their vessels as ships and the modern terminology of referring to keels and sloops as barges, to them, would be somewhat misleading.

The Hull Packet publication sheds light on a few mishaps on the river including one incidence in December, 1848 when widowed father of seven James Moore and Paterson Everett of Winterton, went missing having left Weighton Lock on the north bank on their way to Winteringham, with a cargo of pots. They were never found, though the sails of their vessel were.

In November 1863, a keel belonging to John Fussey of East Halton, was wrecked on Whitton sands. She was carrying a freight of stores and coal for Charles Wells of Hull, much of which was lost. The vessel, however was helped into Winteringham Haven by locals.

The waters around Whitton and Winteringham claimed another victim when the steamer Killarney, on its way from Goole to Bruges, ran aground, capsized and filled with water. Fortunately the crew survived but the vessel, which was owned by the Goole Steamship Company stayed in 18ft to 19ft of water near the Whitton lights.

The vessel had made more than 1,000 journeys from Goole and the accident was put down to a loss of steering power. Although she had toppled over the vessel was later raised from the river bed. No-one lost their life.

An early engraving of the ferry at Barton-upon-Humber.

People on one of the summer pleasure cruises which ran on the Humber in the summer months.

A modern day view of Barrow Haven.

Not everyone's idea of fun, but 'monkey man' Mick Maith of the Spider T demonstrates climbing the rigging can be a quick way to sort out a tangle of ropes.

An amphibious craft at Cleethorpes.

Who said commercialism was a modern day phenomenon?

Employees of Clapson's Barton Shipyard, ready to launch the vessel Mafeking, during the days of sail when such vessels, in these parts at least, were known as ships rather than barges. The latter term was more readily applied to later craft with engines and a somewhat flatter deck configuration. Photo: Courtesy: HKSPS. Photo: courtesy, HKSPS, chairman Dave Parker tel 01482 703647.

Fill the pot for the next stew of memories

If you have enjoyed this book, then please help us make its successor equally as interesting by forwarding your memories and photos to Chris Horan, c/o 22 Priory Crescent, Scunthorpe North Lincs, DN17 1HX.

Any photos or memorabilia should be sent accompanied by your name, address, phone details and a suitable envelope for their return. They are sent at your own risk but we will seek to honour their return.

Memories may be sent by email to chris.horan22@virginmedia.com. To meet print requirements attached photos should be at 300dpi across the full size of the photo and greater if it is a small photo.

Finally, this publication would not have been possible without the help of local papers and their archives, local historians and their painstaking research, the dedication of the Humber Keel and Sloop Preservation Society and individual vessel owners who make it possible for us to glimpse back into history. Admire their work, but make a contribution in either monetary terms or by exchange of skills.

Chris Horan.